LONDON
IN LOCKDOWN

DAVID C. RAMZAN

AMBERLEY

First published 2022

Amberley Publishing
The Hill, Stroud,
Gloucestershire, GL5 4EP

www.amberley-books.com

ISBN: 978 1 3981 1001 4 (print)
ISBN: 978 1 3981 1002 1 (ebook)

British Library Cataloguing in Publication Data.
A catalogue record for this book is available from the British Library.

Typeset in 10pt on 13pt Celeste.
Typesetting by SJmagic DESIGN SERVICES, India.
Printed in the UK.

Contents

Introduction

Throughout the year the streets of London are usually crowded with people: commuters heading to and from their place of work during rush hours; tourists and sightseers from far and wide visiting many of the city's historic landmarks, exhibitions and museums; and shoppers who come to spend time browsing in exclusive stores, popular shops and lively markets. London's restaurants, cafés, public houses, theatres, and places of entertainment are busy from the time they open to the time they close, the streets full of joyful revellers at Christmas and New Year, and gathering en masse for a variety of festivals, ceremonies, and parades.

At the beginning of 2020, it was a year much like any other, and London was looking forward to many events and festivities taking place in the capital: Chinese New Year at London's colourful Soho district; St Patrick's Day Parade, the Irish out in force dressed in green; the Feast of St George, when Trafalgar Square turns red and white; the London Marathon, where thousands line the route cheering on athletes and fun runners; Trooping the Colour, Elizabeth II's birthday parade; and many more annual anniversaries, commemorations and ceremonies.

Then a virus, reported in January, swept in from Asia bringing London to a standstill – something most people today would never have experienced before. Although, at first, people carried on as normal, it soon became clear, as the infection rates increased, that action needed to be taken in an attempt to stop the virus spreading. Social distancing and regularly washing hands were the first in a series of measures put in place before London went into lockdown, the busy thoroughfares empty of traffic and famous attractions empty of people.

London in Lockdown explores some of the capital city's historic streets, most famous tourist attractions and well-known landmarks through 2,000 years of London's remarkable, violent, and turbulent history. The contemporary images of a virtually deserted London reflect upon a period that may never be seen again in our lifetime.

1

Pandemic, War and Pestilence

'God shield our Empire from the might. Of war or famine, plague or blight'.
Winston Churchill (1890)

The last major global pandemic occurred in 1918, towards the end of the First World War, when an outbreak of Spanish flu, an unusually deadly strain of influenza, infected around one-third of the world's population. Very few people alive today would have experienced living through this; however, many would have faced similar tough restrictions during the Second World War as those of 2020/21 – food rationing, shop closures and limitations on travel. In spite of the relentless bombing raids during the Blitz and uncertainty of when the conflict would end, the people did their very best to carry on living as normal life as possible.

Unlike the war, when London's streets were empty because of air raids, most people heading for shelters and only emerging after the 'All Clear' siren sounded, when the first Covid-19 lockdown was introduced during March 2020, the government advising people to stay at home to fight the virus and save lives, London's streets had never been as deserted since the days of the Great Plague.

Following the plague, the City of London was devastated by the Great Fire of 1666, where many residents and workers fled the city as the fire took hold. As a result of the Great Fire around a quarter of the city was destroyed. Then after the city was rebuilt, it expanded outwards from the Roman wall, the original boundary of Londinium.

Although there is a long-held belief that London was founded by the Romans, archaeological evidence suggests humans occupied the area 500,000 years ago. The tribes were forced to abandon their settlement and migrate southwards with the coming of the last Ice Age. As the climate warmed, people reinhabited areas along the densely forested Thames Basin, the river separating various tribal lands crossable by way of a ford, probably located near Westminster, where the water was at its shallowest.

By early first century BC, a small trading community had evolved north of the Thames, occupied by the Romans after the third invasion in AD 43. The Romans named the settlement Londinium, derived from the Celtic word *Londinios*, 'the place of the bold one'. Although fortified with a ditch and earth embankments, topped by wooden barricades, in AD 61, Londinium was sacked and burned by Queen Boudicca, ruler of the Iceni tribe, during a rebellion against Roman governance. The Iceni slaughtered London's inhabitants, leaving the city deserted and in ruins. By around AD 200 the Romans had rebuilt the city, surrounded with a more substantially constructed stone wall with gates, defensive towers, and ditches. After a series of attacks from pirates sailing up the Thames, a fortified wall was constructed along the riverside enclosing the city.

When the Romans withdrew from Britain at the beginning of the fifth century, London was abandoned and left deserted. A new community was established outside the old Roman wall, where the River Fleet flowed into the Thames, by Saxons moving eastwards across the country, and by the late sixth century London had become an important centre of commerce.

As many merchants arrived from various trading nations, a mint was founded to produce silver currency for trade, and various goods were imported, including wine, pottery, exotic foods, and spices, with wool and woollen cloth exported in return.

The Saxons who settled within the city walls during the mid-ninth century faced attacks from fearsome Danes, looting and burning down large areas of the city, before an invading force moving in from the north and east of England overran the city to make London a Danish stronghold. Under the leadership of King Alfred the Great and after a decisive victory over the Danes, a treaty made to keep the peace gave the Norsemen the right to retain kingdoms in the north and east, along with London. Although the treaty brought a period of stability for the people of London, Alfred later took the city by force, expelling the Danes and driving them northwards.

The Anglo-Saxons established a new settlement within the repaired and refortified Roman walls and London flourished once more as a centre of trade. Outside the city wall to the west, Edward the Confessor established an abbey and palace at Westminster, which would later become England's official seat of government.

After William the Conqueror defeated King Harold at Battle in Sussex, he rode into London at the head of his army and was crowned king at Westminster in December 1066. To appease a largely Saxon population William I granted London a charter, giving the inhabitants special rights and privileges, and to keep the city's Saxons under control, as well as protect the city from attack, he ordered the construction of a timber stronghold at the east of the city wall. The fortification was later replaced by a massive stone-built keep, the white-painted fortress and the surrounding defensive walls evolving into the Tower of London.

By the twelfth century, houses were erected outside the old city wall and a new stone Thames crossing to Southwark replaced the wooden London Bridge, which had been rebuilt several times over the previous centuries. A new cathedral dedicated to St Paul the Apostle was built at the north-west of the city to replace an earlier structure, thirteen monasteries were founded, and many parish churches were built. Several markets were established at various locations within and without the city wall – at Cheapside, Leadenhall and Smithfield – and at St Mary's, close to St Paul's Cathedral, one of London's earliest fish markets was founded near the wharfs of Queenhithe and Billingsgate, where fishing vessels unloaded catches.

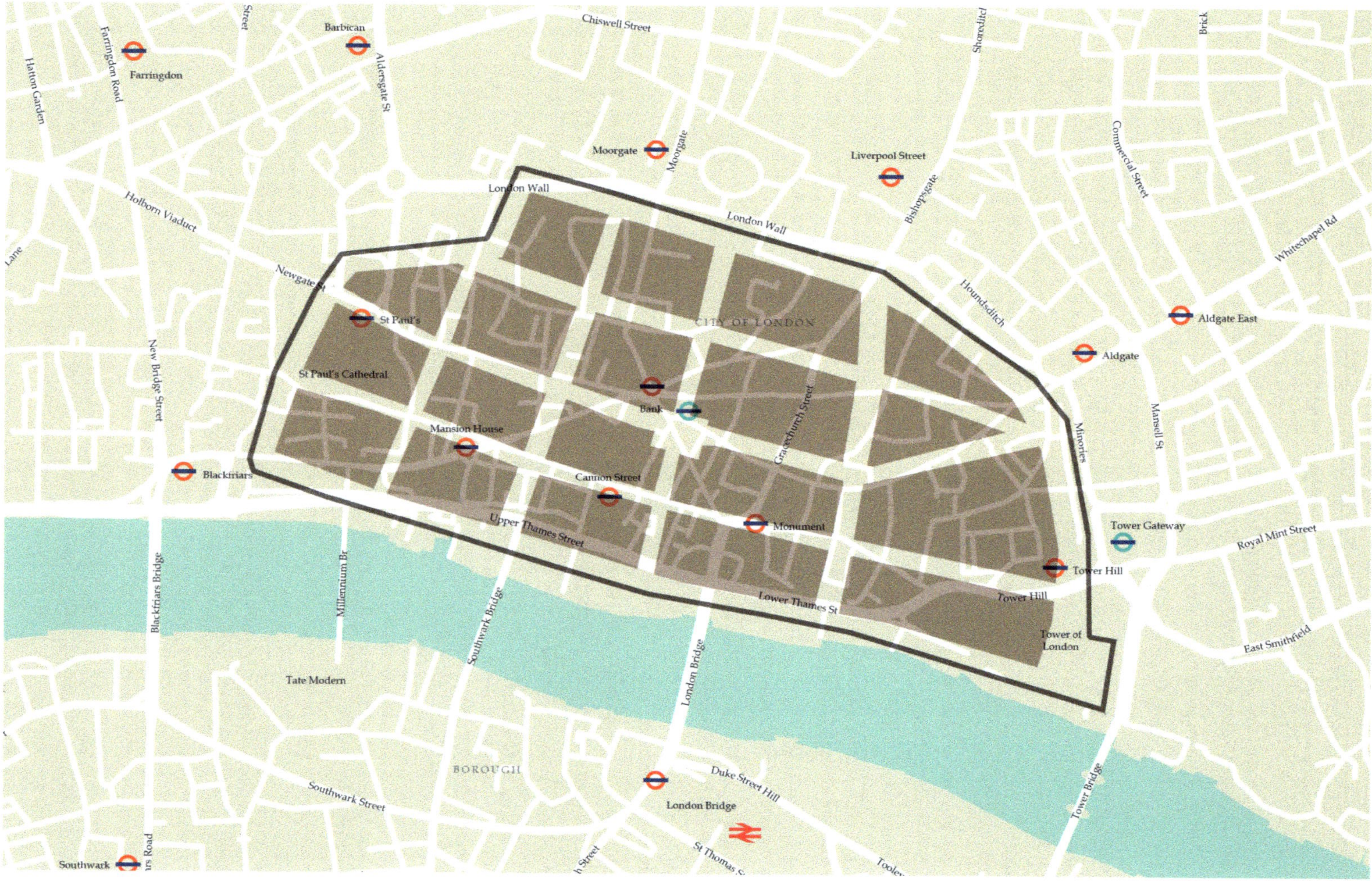

Roman London overlaid on present-day London, from an 1810 plan by antiquary John Britton.

London faced its first case of plague, known as the Black Death, in the autumn of 1348. The loss of life is estimated to have been between 40 and 60 per cent of the entire population, which left London empty and its streets deserted. Although the plague diminished by the end of 1349, another epidemic broke out in 1361, and the deaths resulted in such a shortage of London labourers that rural workers moved to the city to take up their places.

With fewer people available to work the land, peasants demanded an increase in wages to carry out extra work, along with a reduction of taxes and tithes. When the landowner gentry refused their demands, insurrection broke out across the country, and during the late thirteenth century London came under siege from thousands of aggrieved peasants marching on the capital. On crossing London Bridge, the peasants forced their way into the city to sack houses and attacked civic buildings to destroy taxation records.

After occupying the Tower of London, the rebels killed the Archbishop of Canterbury for imprisoning John Ball, a priest sympathetic with their cause. London was held to ransom until one of the rebel leaders, Wat Tyler, was killed by the Lord Mayor of London at Smithfield and the young Richard II promised to agree to their demands, which dispelled the hostile crowd.

During the reign of Elizabeth I, London suffered its worst outbreak of the plaque, between 1563 and 1564, killing around a quarter of the city's population. The queen instructed the government to issue orders through the church to its parishioners to stay in their homes and if any member of the household showed symptoms to remain inside for several weeks after the person had died or recovered. A blue cross was then painted on the front doors of the homes of those afflicted, and bonfires were lit in London's streets in an attempt to clear the corrupted air. The royal court relocated to Windsor Castle, the queen banning movement of goods and people from London to Windsor. Members of the nobility also evacuated the city and Parliament transferred administrative powers to the county town of Hertford until the epidemic had passed.

After Charles I was defeated by the Parliamentarians in the English Civil War and then found guilty of treason, thousands of Londoners turned out to watch the king's execution outside Whitehall Palace in 1649. Under Oliver Cromwell's puritanical regime, however, the people were forced to live by the teachings of the Bible under restrictions, preventing

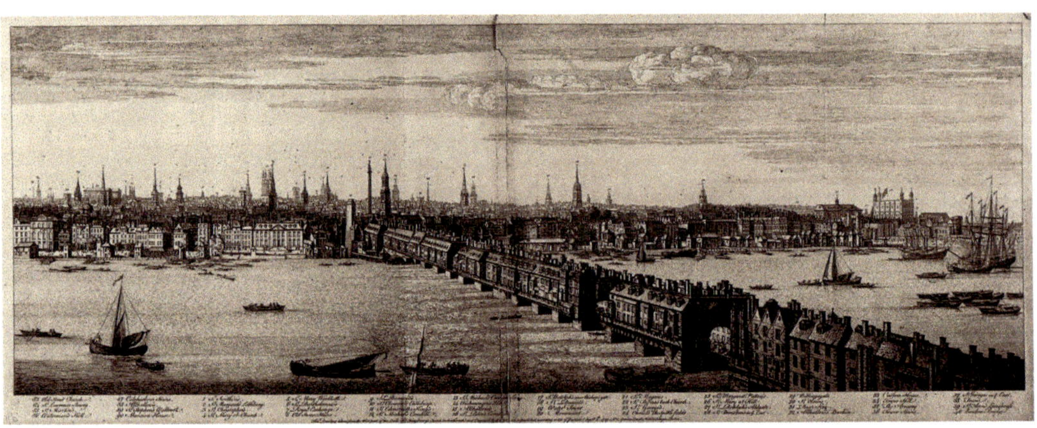

Panorama of the Thames and buildings of the City, mid-1600s. (Wellcome Collection)

them engaging in popular social activities. The inns and theatres were closed, and most sports were banned. People were also forbidden to work on Sundays and were only allowed to go walking on the Lord's day if attending church.

Regulations introduced by Cromwell changed the Christmas festive period as Londoners had once known them – a time of joy, merriment, and eating and feasting with family and friends. A return to conscientious religious celebration was demanded in their place. The display of holly, which had associations with paganism, was banned and soldiers patrolled London's streets, ready to supress unregulated frivolities and confiscate excess food from people's homes. Those found breaking regulations faced severe punishments such as whipping, imprisonment, time in the stocks or a hefty fine. Many Londoners, especially those from the lower social orders, loathed living under the restrictions of a Puritan regime.

After the death of Cromwell and eventual end of governance by the Protectorate, Londoners celebrated the restoration of the monarchy and termination of restrictions – around 20,000 people gathered on the city streets to greet Prince Charles on his return from exile in Europe. Crowned king at Westminster in 1661, under the rule of a sovereign and governed by a newly formed Parliament, London prospered until the plague returned in 1665.

The first outbreak occurred during the spring of 1665, in one of the poorest and most overcrowded parishes outside the city wall, St Giles-in-the-Field. At first, the epidemic spread slowly, forty-three dying by May, but by July just over 17,000 had died. The districts inside and outside the wall, known as liberties, were governed by local administration, where the poor were lacking in any adequate standard of hygiene and open drains flooded the streets already awash with sewage, animal waste, slops, and rubbish. The stench forced people walking the filthy city streets to wear a handkerchief as a mask across their nose and mouth or use nosegays to supress the smell. The common belief was that fleas on rats, which were attracted to the filth and rubbish on the street, were carriers of the plague, but recent studies suggest the bacteria was spread by lice and fleas living on humans.

The Great Plague, as it became known, not only had a devastating effect on London's population (the loss of life estimated to have been up to 100,000, around a quarter of the city's inhabitants), it also had a significant effect on the economy. In an attempt to prevent the disease spreading, boats and ships stopped sailing on the river and all trade with London was halted, resulting in a reduction of goods and produce coming in and going out of the city docks. With people, workers, and tradesmen shut up in their homes, businesses suffered a loss of income, and many people lost their livelihoods. Although parish administrators provided some food, many of London's poor were forced to beg and steal to survive.

In an attempt to defeat the epidemic's spread, London's mayor introduced measures similar to the restrictions recently imposed; taverns, stores, and theatres were shut down, and people were put into quarantine – the word 'quarantine' is taken from the Italian word for 'forty', *quaranta*, a term used for separating people and animals, usually for forty days.

Those caring for plague sufferers wore personal protection such as masks, and the inside of houses, personal effects and goods were washed with vinegar and a lime whitewash, which we now know proves effective in neutralising the bacteria.

By the summer of 1665 many of London's wealthy citizens had fled and Charles II and the royal household relocated to Salisbury, then to Oxford. Parliament was also postponed, relocating to Oxford, along with the court of Westminster. The Lord Mayor of London

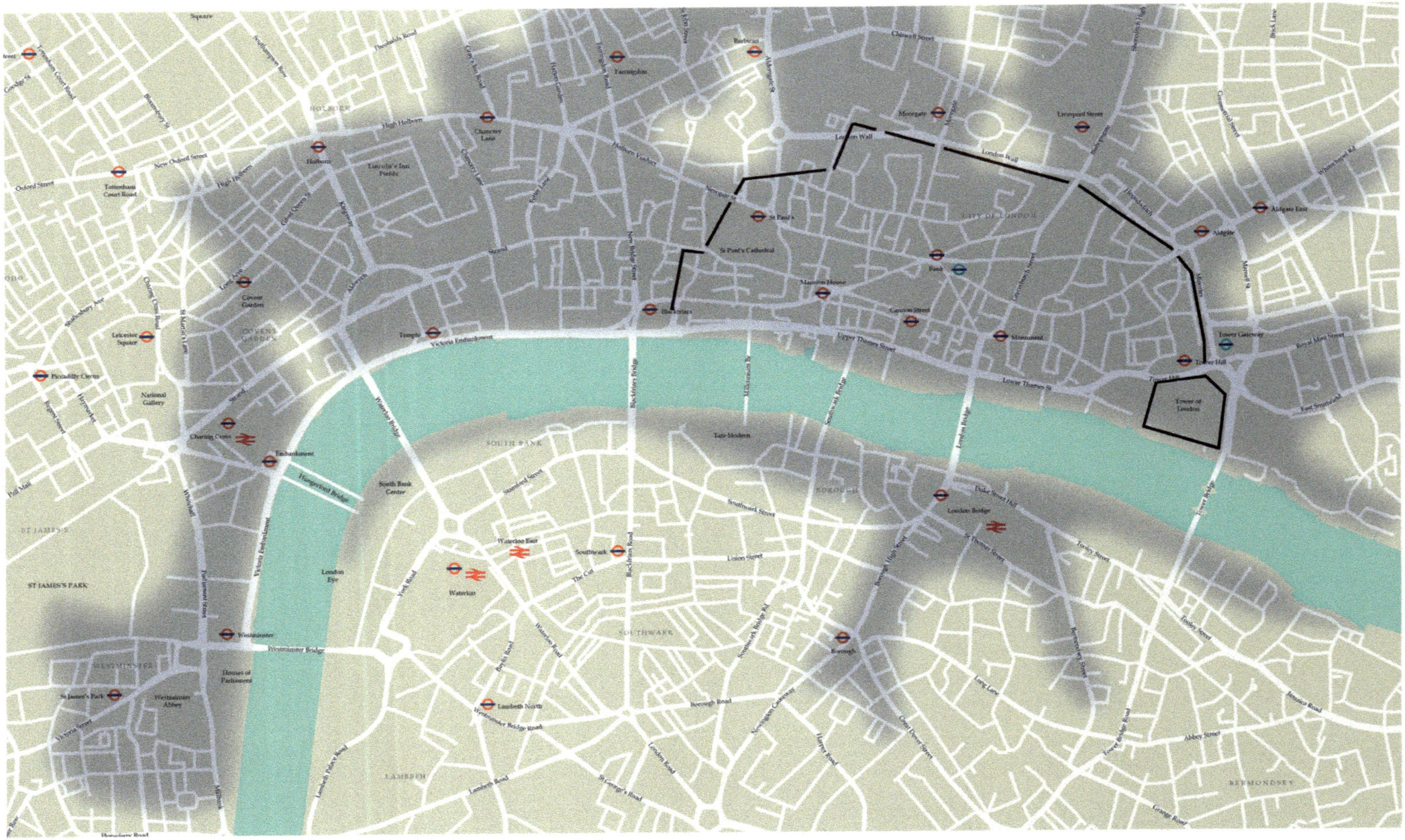

Area showing the spread of the Great Plague, *c.* 1665, overlaid on present-day London.

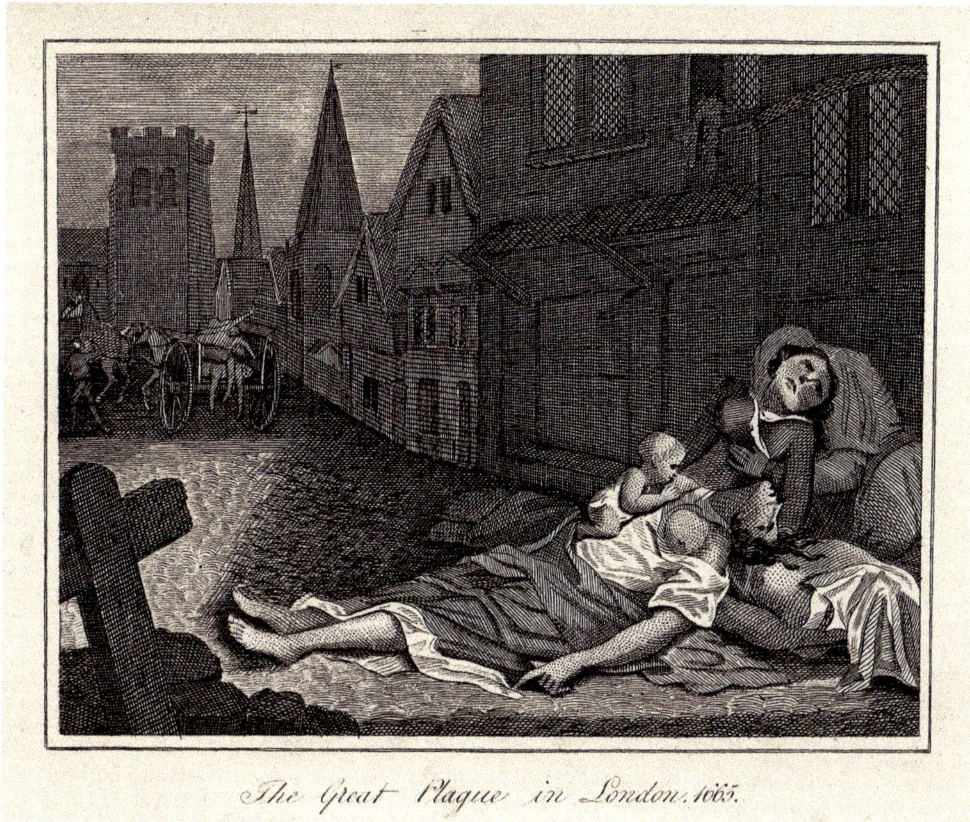

Two women lying dead in a London street during the Great Plague, *c.* 1665. (Wellcome Collection)

and several city aldermen remained to oversee the administration of the city, and a small number of physicians, apothecaries and members of the clergy stayed to care for the needs of infected Londoners.

Those who had no choice but to stay were London's destitute and poor, and those infected were isolated in pest houses or shut up in their homes with a red cross painted on the door. By the late autumn of 1665 the death rate had fallen, and by early 1666 those who fled London – royalty, Members of Parliament, merchants, and the judiciary – gradually returned. Steadily, trade recommenced, and businesses, shops, taverns, and theatres began opening their doors once more

No sooner had London returned to near normal than a fire broke out, in September 1666, at a bakery close to London Bridge. The blaze slowly spread from its source at Pudding Lane, rapidly engulfing large areas of the city as the wind-assisted flames leapt from building to building in the narrow streets.

Where the plague had an adverse effect on the poor and London trade, the Great Fire of London caused the ruin of many city merchants, bankers and property owners, the blaze burning down most of the city's influential commerce and banking district.

Under the guidance of Charles II London was rebuilt, supervised by Surveyor of London Robert Hooke, and although the street plan remained much the same as before, many

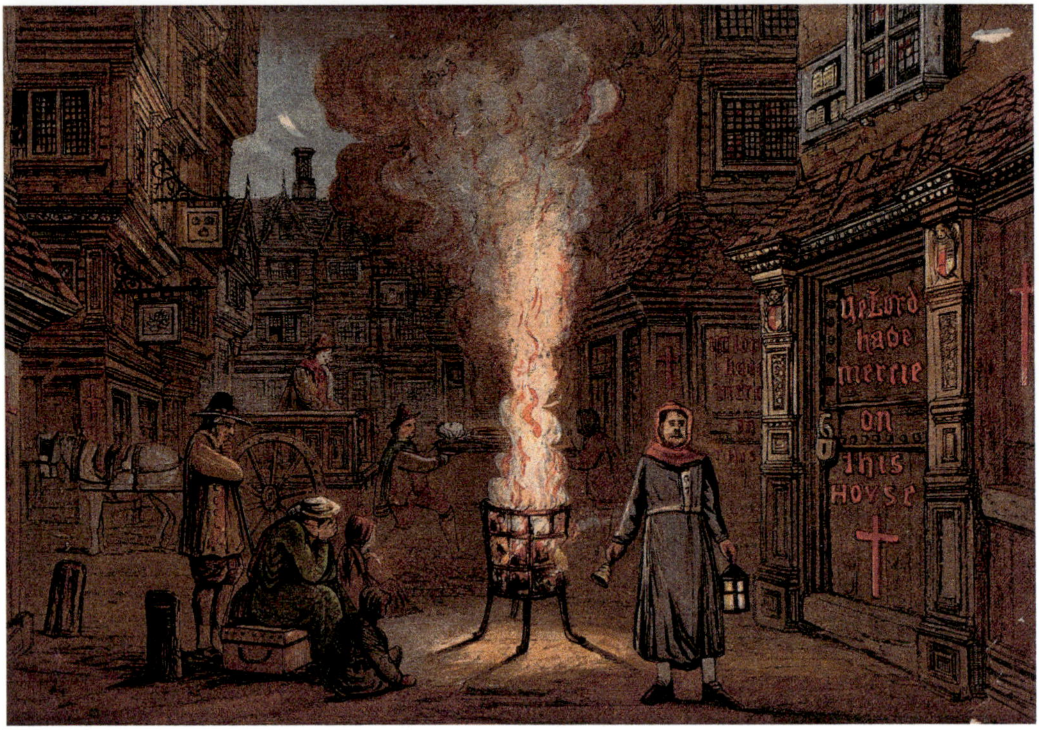

A street during the plague in London. (Engraving by E. Evans 1826–1905; Wellcome Collection)

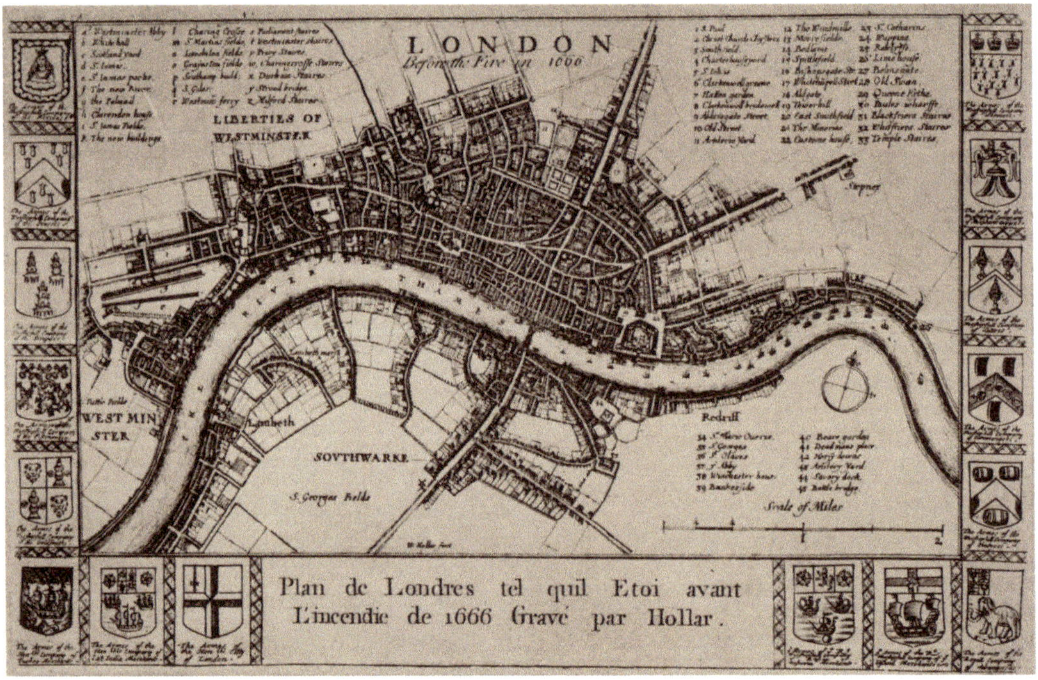

London street plan before the Great Fire, *c.* 1665.

improvements were made, including the widening of the streets, addition of pavements, enclosure of sewers, and controlled and regulated construction of buildings.

The rebuilding took over ten years to complete. The city then rapidly expanded outwards as members of the nobility, wealthy merchants and landowners began developing vacant land to the north and west, building elegant properties and formal squares at Lincoln Inn Fields, St Martin-in-the-Fields and Bloomsbury, with rows of tall properties erected along the Strand, around Covent Garden, Soho and Mayfair. Sir Christopher Wren was commissioned to design and build the new St Paul's Cathedral (the previous cathedral was destroyed in the fire), and a majority of the old Roman city wall was demolished to make way for new roads and buildings.

During the redevelopment the surviving houses, shops, and gatehouses on London Bridge were demolished, making access to and from the city free-flowing, and over the following two centuries, to link with rapidly expanding communities to the south of the Thames, several new bridges were erected.

Through an increase in trade, commerce, working practices, and employment opportunities, the population of London climbed from just under 1 million in 1800 to 6 million by the end of that century. The rise in population and the unhygienic standard of living in London slums resulted in a series of cholera outbreaks during the mid-nineteenth century. One of the worst occurred in Soho during 1854, a district of overcrowded slum tenements and an inefficient sanitary system.

Cholera killed over 14,000 Londoners, the disease believed at the time to have been spread by bad smells and contaminated air. To eradicate the epidemic streets in affected areas were washed down and the local authority advised people to improve ventilation by opening windows and doors to let fresh air in and keep themselves and their houses clean. The population was also advised to restrict all movement outside the home and to place themselves into quarantine if they became infected.

Through research carried out by physicians such as John Snow, it was eventually discovered cholera was transmitted by a waterborne infection – the water from standpipes contaminated by sewerage seeping into the water supply.

The cholera outbreaks forced the government into making improvements to London's drainage and sewerage system. The Metropolitan Board of Works were tasked with joining up the existing patchwork of systems and formed a plan to create a modern network of sewers under London's streets, directing waste into the Thames.

Although outbreaks of cholera subsided by the end of the nineteenth century, Londoners were about to face another threat, this time from overseas. War broke out in Europe and the city became a primary target during Germany's First World War bombing campaign. On 31 May 1915, as Londoners were asleep in their beds, a Zeppelin dropped ninety incendiary bombs and thirty grenades onto the city. The explosions and fire caused the death of seven people and injured thirty-five, spreading panic among the city's population, who had come under airborne attack for the first time in London's history.

After this first attack the air raids continued. The only early warning of an impending raid came from policeman riding bikes through London's streets, blowing whistles as a warning to take cover. In September 1915, a Zeppelin passing over the city dropped a 3-ton bomb on the city's financial district. Narrowly missing St Bartholomew's Hospital, the bomb exploded at Bartholomew's Close, damaging buildings and tearing an 8-foot crater in the ground.

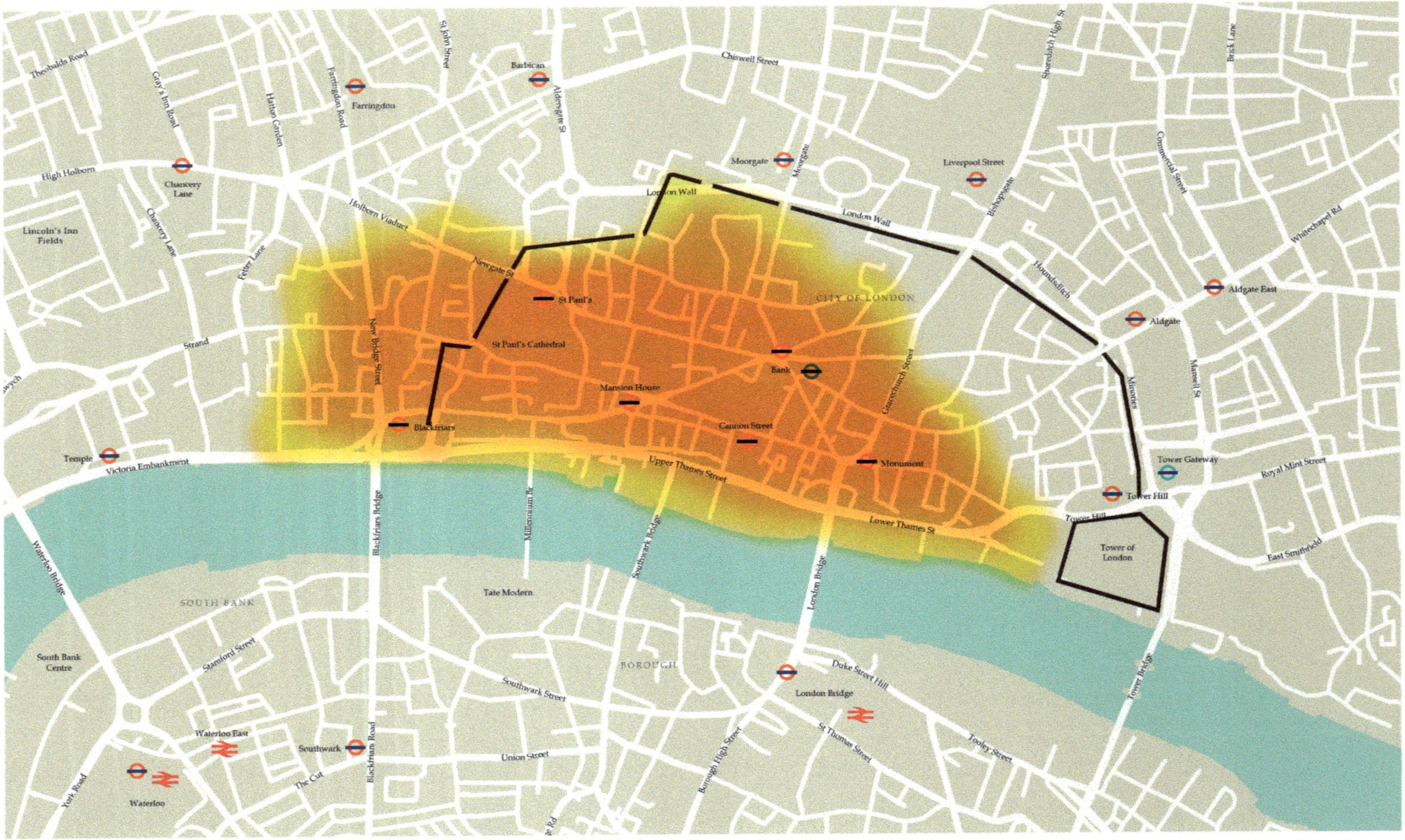

Area showing the spread of the Great Fire in 1666, overlaid on present-day London.

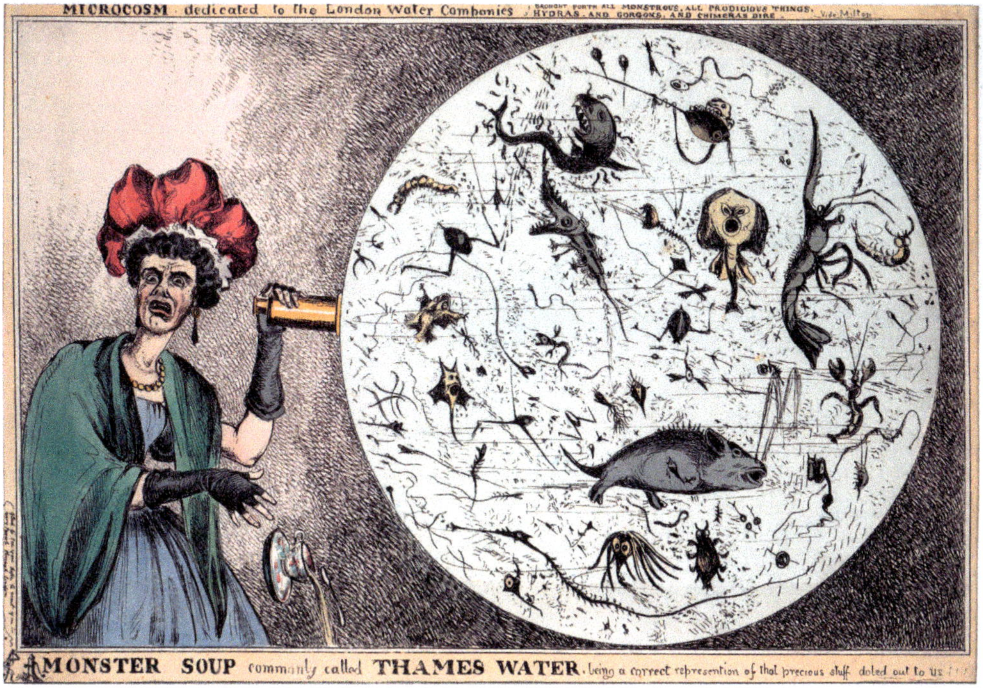

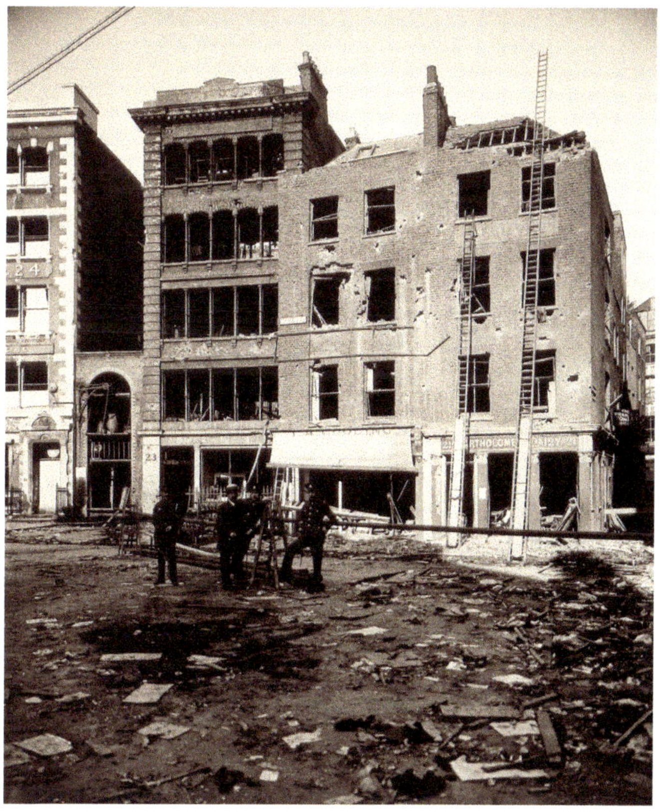

Above: Woman discovering the monstrous contents of a magnified drop of the Thames. (W. Heath, 1828; Wellcome Collection)

Right: Bartholomew Close after the Zeppelin air raid in 1915. (Wellcome Collection)

Although blackouts were introduced early in the war, when street lamps were turned off or dimmed and heavy curtains were pulled across windows at night to cut out light that could be seen from above, the public demanded more protection against raids. The government recalled anti-aircraft guns from the frontline in France and positioned powerful searchlights around the city. The first daytime raid on London, carried out by biplane bomber aircraft in June 1917, resulted in the death of 162 people. By the end of the war it's estimated the city's casualties numbered 667 killed and almost 2,000 wounded.

Two decades later and London faced the terror of another aerial bombing campaign after the beginning of the Second World War. On this occasion, the government had already made plans to evacuate around 4 million people, mostly women and children, from the city to the countryside. Once again a blackout was introduced, to ensure enemy aircraft could not see the lights of the city at night. And every time people left their homes they were required to carry a gas mask, for fear of aerial poison gas attacks. With street lamps either turned off, dimmed, or shielded so the light shone downward, and with vehicle headlamps and traffic signals also shielded, people making their way about London streets found it particularly difficult. Although the government threatened to punish people for not carrying a gas mask, it was never made a legal requirement; however, anyone breaking blackout regulations faced severe penalties. The blackout was one of many unpleasant restrictions people were forced to live by; another was food rationing.

Before the war around 70 per cent of Britain's food and livestock feed was imported from overseas. When many supply ships were sunk travelling in convoys targeted by Germany's Kriegsmarine, it caused a shortage of most of the necessities required to survive. The government introduced a system of rationing. Everyone was issued with a ration book, ensuring people only received an equal proportion of the goods available in the shops and preventing the hoarding of goods, which left a shortage of the essentials for others. Most food was rationed, apart from fruit and vegetables, and as shortages increased long queues formed outside shops and grocers. Although most people did not have cars, petrol was also rationed, and vehicles were immobilised when not in use to prevent the enemy using them if the country was invaded. Rationing created a black market where unscrupulous shopkeepers sold extra produce at inflated prices from 'under the counter', and petty criminals, known as 'spivs', were ready to fill a gap in the market selling a variety of misappropriated and stolen goods and luxury items. Those caught dealing in black market goods faced prosecution, even for the most minor of offences.

The sustained bombing campaign between 1940 and 1941, known as the Blitz, was intended to not only to destroy and disrupt London's industry, but it was also an attempt to break the spirit of the people. By the war's end, just under 30,000 people in London had been killed during bombing raids. On 29 December 1940, London suffered the worse night of the Blitz, when the first wave of German aircraft dropped more than 10,000 incendiaries over a targeted area of the city, with St Paul's Cathedral at its centre, the beginning of the second great fire of London. As large aeras of London burned, the following wave of bombers, using the fires as a beacon, dropped multiple payloads of 550-Ib high-explosive bombs down upon the buildings and people below. With London's firefighters struggling to contain the blaze, the city was saved from almost total destruction when bad weather over the Channel prevented Germany's third bomber wave taking off.

During these prolonged air raids, London's Underground stations became mass air-raid shelters, and as people became more used to sheltering in the Underground, they started taking their own bedding, tea, food, and other home comforts with them, forming little communities, playing card games, and singing songs to try and keep their spirits up as the bombs fell in the streets above. As soon as the 'all clear' sounded, people re-emerged from the depths of the Underground to get back on with their lives.

Although few people had televisions, all broadcasts were cancelled, and cinemas, theatres, dance halls, museums, and sports venues were closed down. While most public houses stayed open, there were drink restrictions; beer was plentiful, but there was a shortage of spirits. Within a few weeks the wartime lockdown ended. Musicals, shows, and reviews returned to London theatres, and cinemas opened their doors to the public once more. Going to the theatre, cinema or pub was one way Londoners and military personnel on leave were able to find some escape from the rigours of war.

Of all the spectator sports football was by far the most popular, and when regionalised football competition recommenced after the league shut down, fans returned in reduced numbers – much like during Covid. Restrictions on attendances were made to allow safe evacuation if there was an air raid. During the first year of the war attendances were low, a match averaging around 2,000 or 3,000; however, towards the war's end numbers had almost quadrupled.

Although people had to endure travel restrictions (due to a lack of petrol to run domestic vehicles and a reduction of some trains, which were reassigned for troop carrying), people commuted to work as trains, trams, buses, and Underground services ran throughout the war.

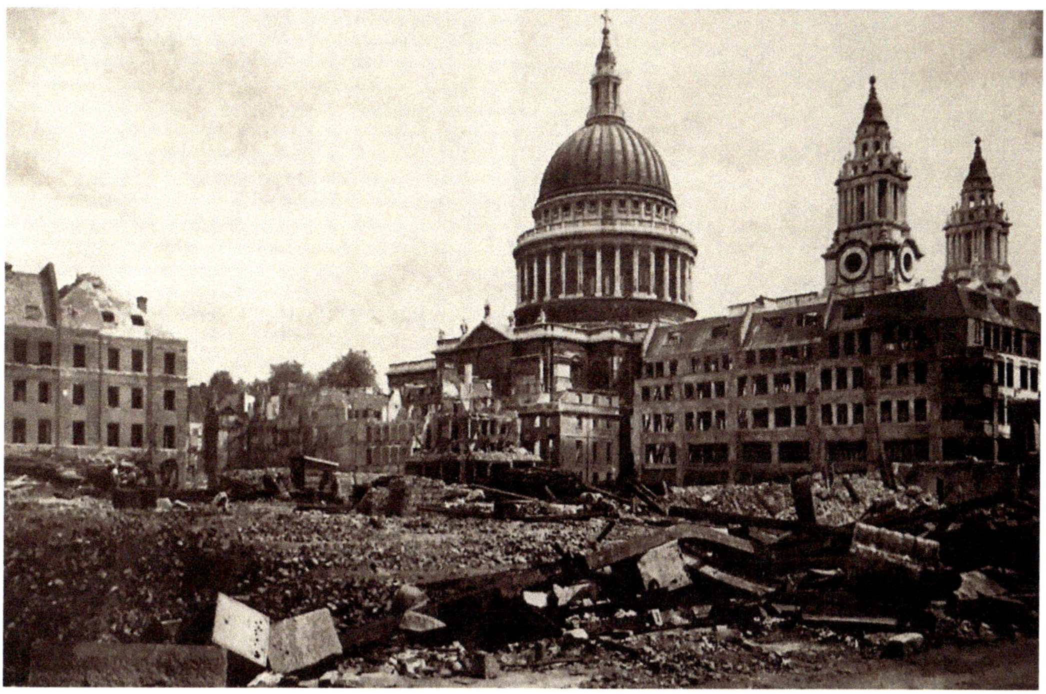

Paternoster Row after an air raid during the Second World War.

Since the war years, London and its population have faced many other periods of adversity. In a struggle for independence and home rule, Irish republicans carried out acts of sabotage in the capital between the 1970s and 1990s, planting explosives at stations, army barracks, department stores, exhibitions, car parks, on trains and buses, even in postboxes, causing death and horrific injuries to many people going about their daily routine.

Around the same time as the bombing campaign, the country was crippled by strikes and an economic downturn. In an attempt to reduce commercial electricity consumption, the result of industrial action by coal miners and the effects of a global oil crises, the government introduced a three-day working week. Television broadcast restrictions were brought into force, only suspended during Christmas and New Year, and the use of electricity to heat shops and restaurants was banned.

Most of London's public houses closed and, with petrol in short supply, it became increasingly difficult for people travelling outside of their local area to meet with friends and relations. Those able to travel into London during power cuts worked in offices by the light of portable lamps. Nevertheless, much like the Blitz, the people got on with it the best as possible under threat of explosions and the many restrictions they faced.

More recently, London has suffered from various acts of terrorism, with attacks carried out by terrorist groups or individuals, all of which had long-term social and economic implications for the city and the people. The consequence of these terrorist actions has resulted in a higher presence of armed police on London's streets and a ring of steel erected around central London, with road closures, barriers placed along the length of Thames bridges, separating traffic from pedestrians, and barricades and bollards positioned at strategic places throughout the capital to protect its buildings and people from attack.

Then, in January 2020, Britain faced its worst crises in post-wars years when a new deadly strain of coronavirus, originating from Wuhan, China, arrived, believed to have first been transmitted from animals to humans in December 2019. By mid-January the virus had rapidly spread throughout China and within three months it had become a worldwide pandemic, the deaths from the virus surging past 11,000 globally. It is estimated that by March 2020 the number of cases worldwide had passed 3.25 million, with over 36,000 thousand dying.

In an attempt to control the spread in Britain, the government released their 'Covid-19 Action Plan', advising the public to regularly wash their hands, keep 2 metres from people and avoid non-essential travel. Restrictions prevented people mixing socially at public houses, restaurants, theatres and cinemas, and anyone with a continuous cough or fever were advised to self-isolate. As cases increased by late March, the government introduced 'lockdown'. A majority of schools were closed, along with public venues, restaurants, theatres, museums, cinemas, public houses, and sports arenas. As more research on the spread of the virus was carried out, it became compulsory to wear a face mask in shops and on public transport or in other public spaces. Although cases fell during the summer months, a significant increase in August and September resulted in the introduction of varying levels of lockdown across Britain from October and onwards into 2021.

The photographs of London in lockdown show this ancient and historic city as it has never been seen before. This pictorial journey through London's streets takes in the areas affected by the Great Plague and the Great Fire of London, and districts and landmarks outside the old city limits to the west, where many of the city's most wealthy made their escape.

2

City on Fire

'I went againe to the ruins, for it was no longer a Citty.'
John Evelyn (1666)

Not long after midnight, on Sunday 2 September 1666, a small fire broke out in a bakery on Pudding Lane, which eventually spread across the City of London, causing one of the most catastrophic events in its history. The view from Lower Thames Street shows an empty Monument Street, where tourists would normally gather around the memorial designed by Sir Christopher Wren to commemorate the Great Fire of London, erected close to where the fire started on that fateful night. The lane was said to be named after animal puddings – a medieval word for guts and entrails – transported down from butchers' shops at Eastcheap to the dung barges on the Thames.

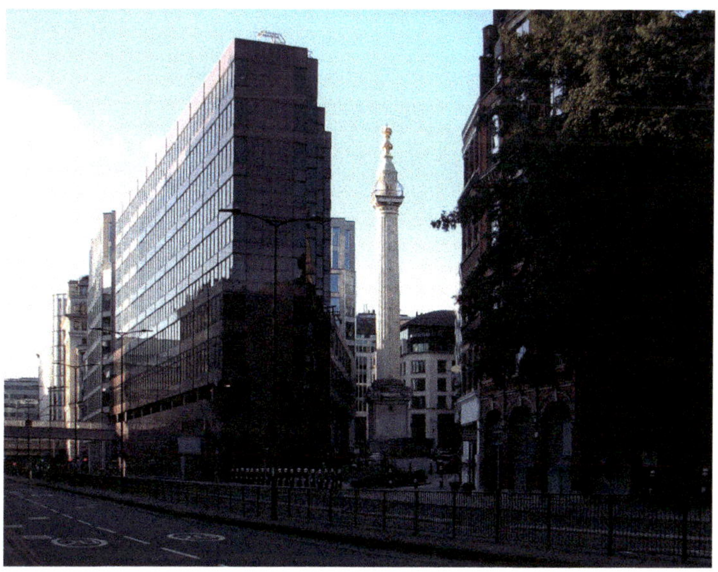

Monument Street, EC3.

Erected between 1671 and 1677, the Monument measures 202 feet high with a viewing gallery at the top, accessed by a spiral staircase consisting of 311 steps. After several people committed suicide by leaping from the top, the gallery was enclosed by a cage in 1842.

St Margaret's on Fish Street was the first church lost to the Great Fire, one of eighty-seven churches destroyed in the blaze, situated where the Monument stands today. Close by was St Michael's at Crooked Lane, within the parish where the first cases of the plague occurred within the city wall the previous year. Although also burned down, the church was rebuilt by Sir Christopher Wren in 1687 as part of London's redevelopment programme after the fire.

Crooked Lane took its name from the way the thoroughfare's route ran in diagonals from Great Eastcheap to Fish Street Hill, towards London Bridge. After a new road layout was proposed as an approach to London Bridge in the early 1800s, St Michael's Church and many properties, including those on Crooked Lane, were demolished to make way for King William Street, named after the reigning monarch.

The city's first Underground station terminus, King William Street, situated at the street's southern end, had a relatively short life. Opening in November 1890, the station had closed within six years after changes to the railway system. With no trains running on the line, the tracks were removed and the station was blocked up during the First World War, in fear the tunnel might be used by enemy agents. The tunnel was then converted into a deep, underground air-raid shelter, which was used throughout the Second World War.

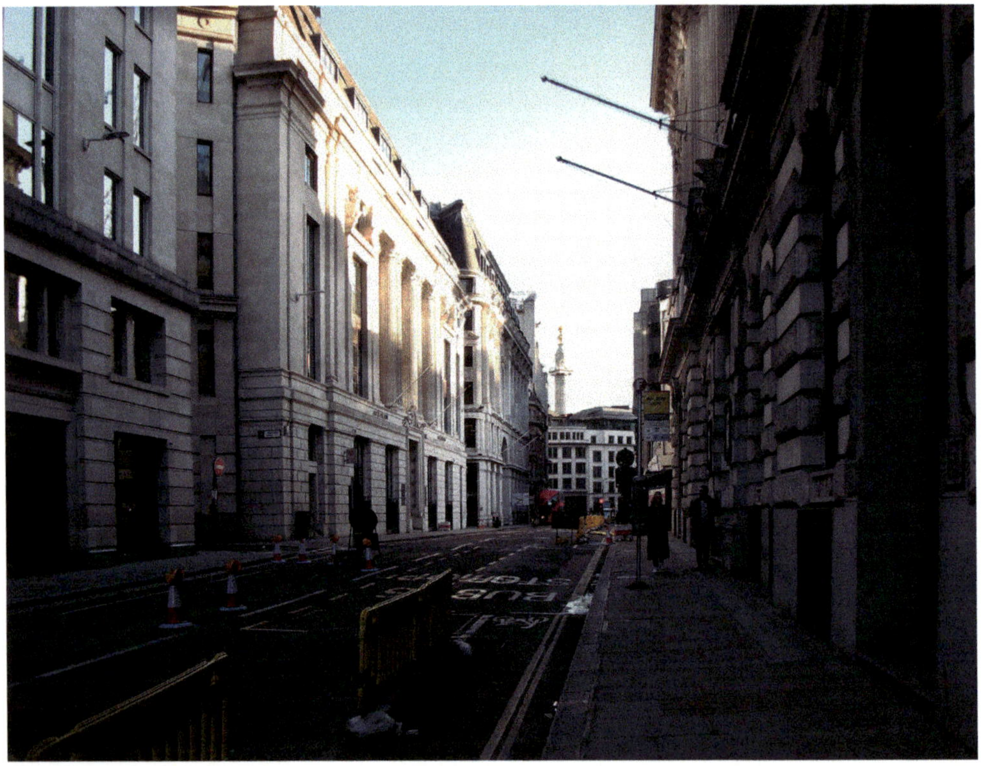

King William Street, EC4.

King William Street, one of the major routes running out from London's historic financial centre, is usually busy with pedestrians making their way to and from their offices and buses and black cabs transporting workers about the city.

As the blaze spread out from Pudding Lane, parish constables wanted to pull down houses on adjoining streets to stop the fire spreading, but were stopped from doing so by the Lord Mayor, Sir Thomas Bloodworth, believing the fire was not that serious, remarking, 'A woman could piss it out.'

By morning the fire had spread towards the river, burning down several more churches, including one on Lovat Lane to the east. Once known as Love Lane, possibly because of the many prostitutes who plied their trade in the narrow passageway, the name was changed to Lovat (after Lord Lovat) to avoid confusion with the Love Lane situated behind the City of London Guildhall.

Salmon from Lord Lovat's fisheries was landed by boats at Billingsgate Dock, and the Company of Fishmongers suggested the name change in 1939. Halfway along the lane to the north is St Mary-at-Hill. This seventeenth-century church, designed by Sir Christopher Wren with works carried out by Robert Hooke, was erected at the site of a twelfth-century

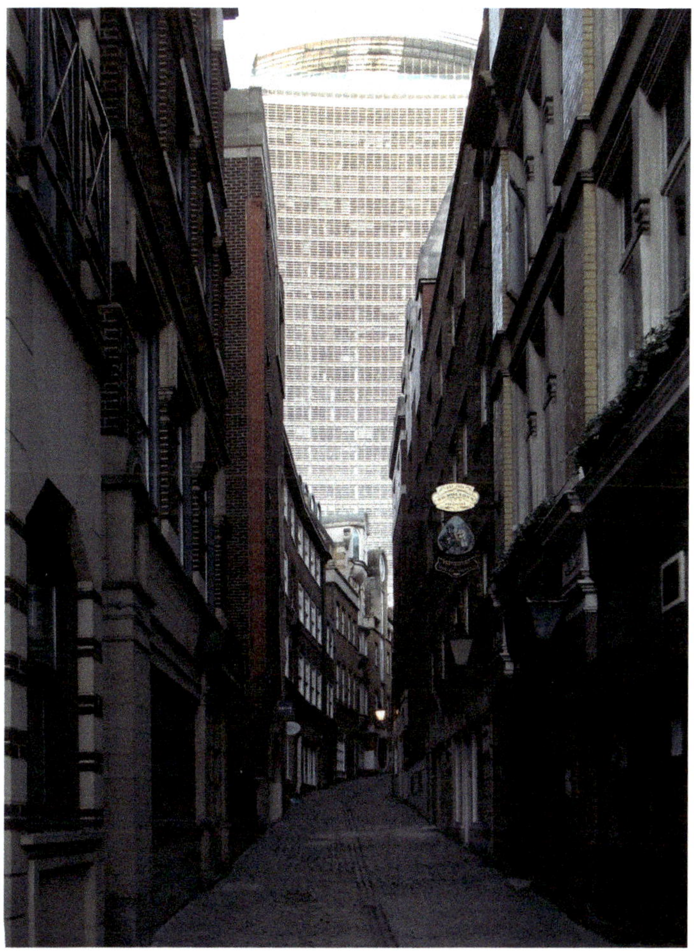

Lovat Lane, EC3.

church that had been severely damaged during the Great Fire. Although surviving the Blitz, the church was restored after being extensively damaged by fire in 1988.

Much of the modern-day financial district of the city has been rebuilt several times since the Great Fire. Streets have been altered and rerouted to accommodate large regeneration projects, specifically after the Second World War, when many of the city's buildings were destroyed by bombing. Queen Victoria Street, cutting through from Blackfriars to the Bank of England, was built when the District Line, running directly below, was constructed between 1867 and 1871.

At the eastern end is the Blackfriars public house, built in the late 1800s on the site of a medieval Dominican friary. Once a thriving friary community, as their numbers dwindled during the mid-1500s, the friary buildings were let and then sold off, with one converted into the Blackfriars Theatre. Retaining its liberties granted by Henry VIII, James Burbage erected a new theatre on the site of the original without acquiring permission – Blackfriars was outside the jurisdiction of London's civic authority.

Shakespeare's company, the King's Men, performed at Blackfriars Theatre. The playwright purchased lodgings at St Andrew's Hill, off present-day Queen Victoria Street. Blackfriars was one of several theatres closed down by the Puritans after the English Civil War; it was later demolished in 1655.

Botolph Lane takes its name from St Botolph Billingsgate, another church destroyed in the Great Fire. At the opposite end stood St George Botolph Lane, backing onto Pudding

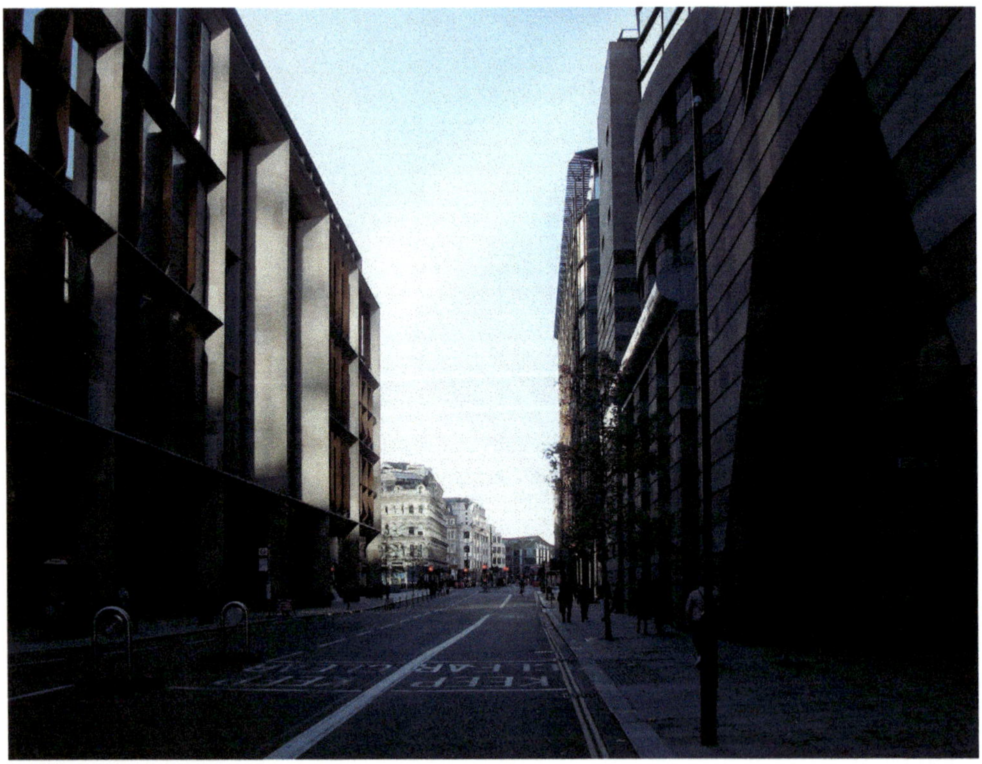

Queen Victoria Street, EC4.

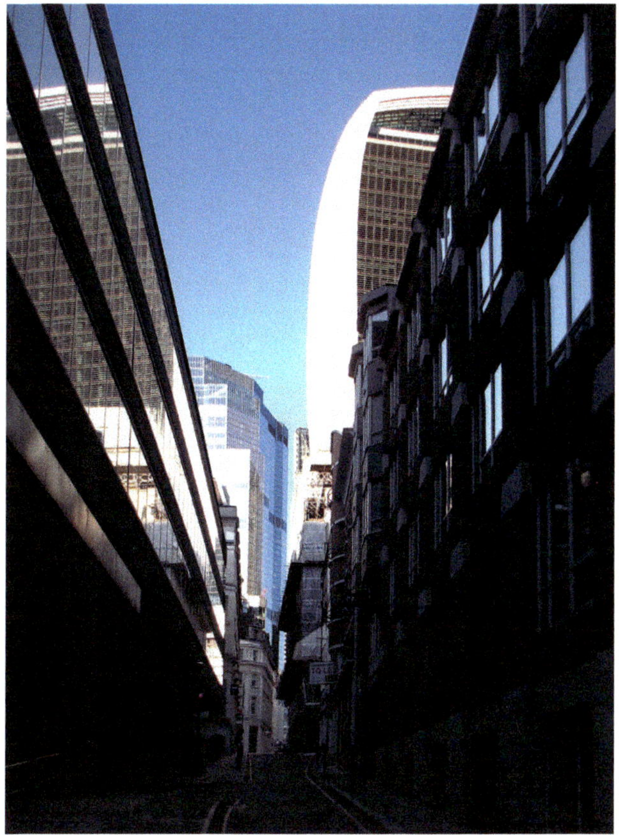

Botolph Lane, EC3.

Lane. The church was one of the fifty-one rebuilt by the office of Sir Christopher Wren. After the major rebuilding programme was completed, the two parishes serving the district, St Botolph Billingsgate and St George Botolph Lane, were combined.

While overseeing the building of St Paul's Cathedral it is believed Christopher Wren resided at a house on Botolph Lane, which was demolished in 1906, two years after St George Botolph Lane was also taken down after falling into decay. Churches dedicated to St Botolph, the Anglo-Saxon patron saint of travellers, were usually built at city gates. The three surviving London churches named after St Botolph are located at Aldgate, Aldersgate, and Bishopsgate.

As the fire took hold, moving towards the river and the Tower of London, even though the high, solid curtain wall around the fortress offered some protection, buildings surrounding the tower were blown up to make a firebreak. It has been estimated around 600,000 lbs of gunpowder were stored in the White Tower at the time of the fire, and if ignited the explosion would not only have destroyed the tower, but many buildings for several miles around, as well as all the ships moored adjacent on the Thames.

As the fire crept closer every effort was made to load the barrels of gunpowder onto ships and transport them safely downstream. William I had ordered the building of a temporary stronghold to the east of the Roman city wall 600 years before the Great Fire. Later built in stone, and after additions to the fortress were made by a succession of monarchs, Edward I enclosed the tower behind a defensive outer wall.

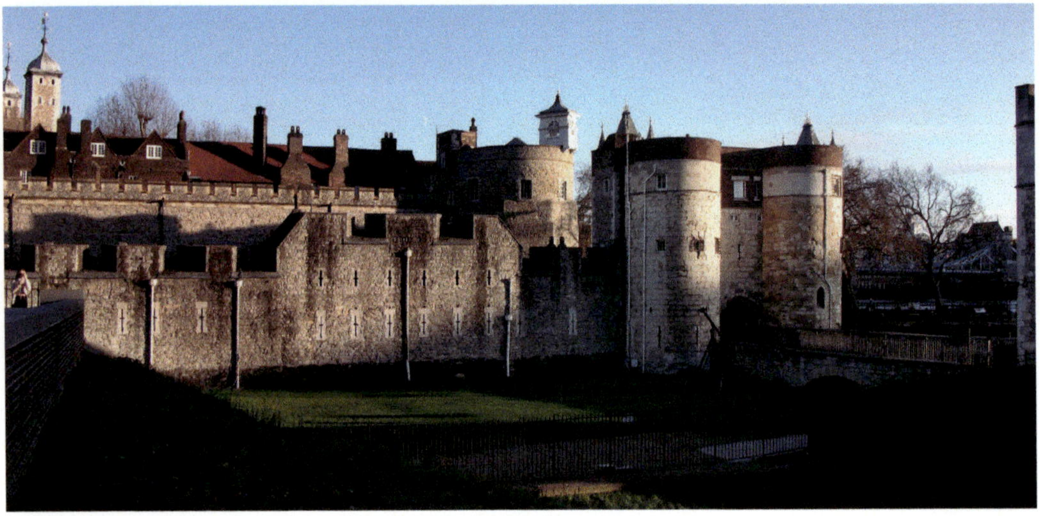

Tower of London, EC3.

The scene of many conflicts, the Tower of London was attacked and occupied during the Peasants' Revolt in 1381, and during a time of civil unrest in 1841 the Constable of the Tower, the Duke of Wellington, strengthened its defences when the government feared rioting and revolution, and transformed the Tower Yeoman Warders, a disorderly lot by all accounts, into a much more professional unit.

The Tower played an important role in both the First and Second world wars, as a training camp, barracks, and prison. Twelve spies were executed at the Tower, and Rudolph Hess, a leading member of the Nazi Party, was briefly held in custody there, charged with war crimes. The Tower's moat was converted into an allotment after the government urged the public to 'Dig for Victory', calling for green spaces to be used as vegetable plots to supplement rations.

Although an inflatable barrage balloon flew above the fortress to deter attack from low flying aircraft, high-explosive bombs fell on the fortification, destroying sections of the mint, the old hospital block, and the North Bastion.

The Tower of London remains a working fortress and Royal Palace and is one of London's most popular tourist attractions – over 3 million people visit annually. It has only ever had to close during the war and for four days annually over Christmas, but when London went into lockdown the Tower's gates closed to the public, staying this way until May 2021.

In December 1564, the occupants of thirty-six properties in Cornhill, a majority drapers and clothworkers, were given notice to vacate their premises by the following March, as the site was to be acquired for building London's first stock exchange. Established by Sir Thomas Gresham and modelled on the Bourse Exchange in Antwerp, the Royal Exchange was officially opened in 1571 by Elizabeth I, who awarded it a royal title and a licence to sell alcohol.

Set out as a square with an open courtyard at the centre, Gresham added two stories above the trading floor, rented out to various retailers. The exchange, however, soon became notorious as a place where the idle gathered and unsolicited women offering fruit for sale at the gate swore at passers-by. The rowdy stockbrokers were banned from

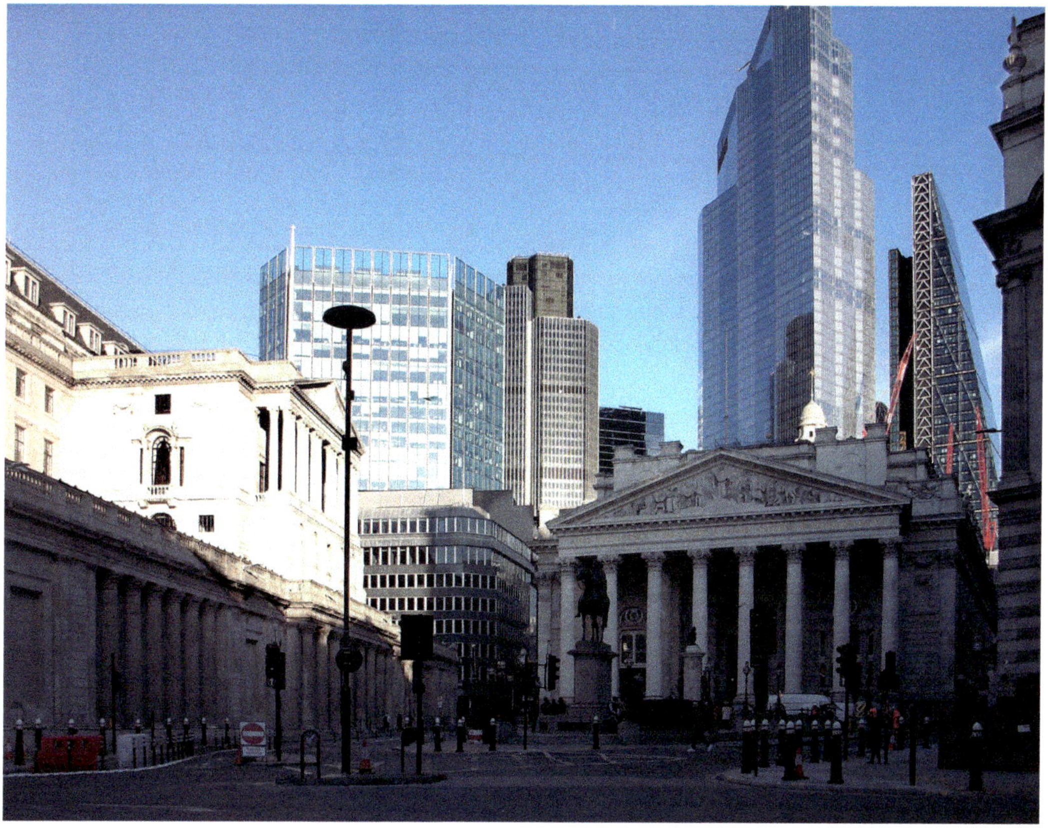

Royal Exchange, EC3.

entering the exchange because of their unacceptable manners and were made to carry out transactions in adjacent establishments.

When the Great Fire reached Cornhill, the flames swept through the Royal Exchange galleries and its courts, gutting and destroying the building. A new, slightly larger, exchange was built on the site after plans to relocate to Queenhithe on the Thames were rejected. Areas of the exchange building were once again let to shops and businesses, including Lloyd's and the East India Company.

A fire, thought to have started in the Lloyd's Rooms in January 1838, destroyed the second exchange, which was replaced by the current building, designed by William Tite and opened by Queen Victoria in 1844. One of the city's historic buildings to survive the Blitz, the Royal Exchange was let to various banking and financial institutions. After being refurbished during the 1980s and remodelled in the 2000s, retailers, boutiques, restaurants, shops and cafés occupy the courtyard and surrounding spaces and, as with many places where people gather socially, had closed during lockdown in 2020.

Opposite the Royal Exchange is the Bank of England, an institution formed to act as the government's bank in 1694. The building on Threadneedle Street has been the headquarters of the bank since 1734, and over time acquired adjacent properties, until the bank owned the whole 3.5-acre site.

After several extensions were added the bank was demolished. A new building was completed in 1939, just as war broke out in Europe. Although the Bank of England survived direct hits during the Blitz, the Nazi regime attempted to destabilise the British economy by introducing forged notes into the country, reported to have a face value of £134 million.

The Bank of England introduced a new, blue £1 note that included a metal thread running through the linen as an attempt to stop forgery, the first time such a method had been used, and withdrew all banknotes with a greater value of £5.

At the time of the Great Fire a majority the properties on streets that make up the present financial centre were constructed mostly of timber with wattle-and-daub walls and overhanging galleries, all crammed side by side between grand houses and administrative buildings.

The tradespeople working and living in the district – carpenters, leather workers, candle makers, milliners, and bakers – belonged to the city's many guilds and livery companies.

To the east of the Bank of England, the medieval route known as Soper Lane is reputed to have been where soap makers and sellers lived in the early twelfth century, when soap was only made in Bristol and London. The lane was adopted as the main road through the city for the Lord Mayor's procession and the monarch's coronation route from the Tower to Westminster.

The soap makers' workshops were then occupied by a community of women workers, converting raw silk into yarn for weaving and making cords, ribbons, and laces. After ravaged by the Great Fire, Soper Lane was rebuilt and renamed Queen Street in honour of Catherine of Braganza, wife of Charles II. King Street, running to the north, was built in conjunction with Queen Street to form a direct route from the river to the Guildhall, the City of London's Town Hall, erected on the site of a Roman amphitheatre.

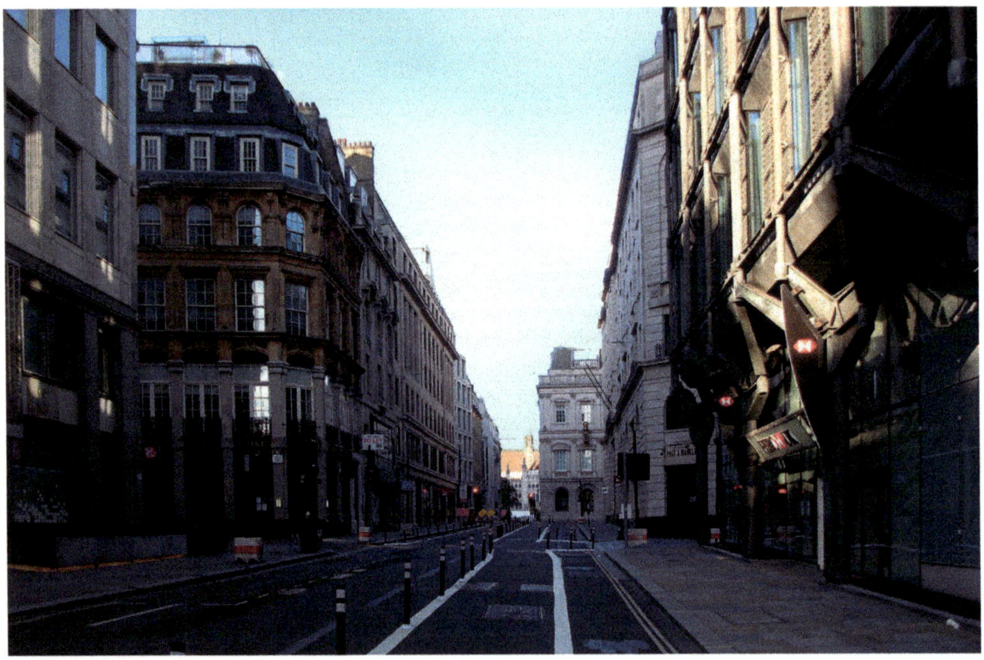

Queen Street, EC4.

Although suffering damage in the Great Fire, the fifteenth-century Town Hall was restored, and a grand entrance added in 1788. The Guildhall's original roof was rebuilt in 1954 after it was destroyed during the Blitz.

Know previously as Cordwainer Street, after the shoemakers who once worked there, and then Hosier Street, after the hosiers who followed, Bow Lane runs north from Mansion House to the sixteenth-century St Mary-le-Bow Church, rebuilt after the Great Fire. The parish of Mary-le-Bow was one of the more densely populated within the city walls, where mortality during the plague was extremely high.

It is said that those born within the sound of the church's bells can call themselves London cockneys. Legend also has it that Dick Whittington, down on his luck and leaving London, heard the bells calling him back, prophesising he would become Lord Mayor.

To the west of the upper part of Bow Lane is Williamson's Tavern, the former residence of London's Lord Mayors, believed to hold the oldest excise licence in the city and rumoured to be haunted by the ghost of a woman known as Martha – the cellar bar is named after her. Bow Lane is intersected by Watling Street, taking its name from an ancient route running from Dover through London to St Albans.

The Great Fire reached as far north as the London Wall at the old Moorgate, which led out onto moorland, from which the gate acquired its name. To the north was an area known as Finsbury Fields, outside the city wall, where hastily prepared unconsecrated

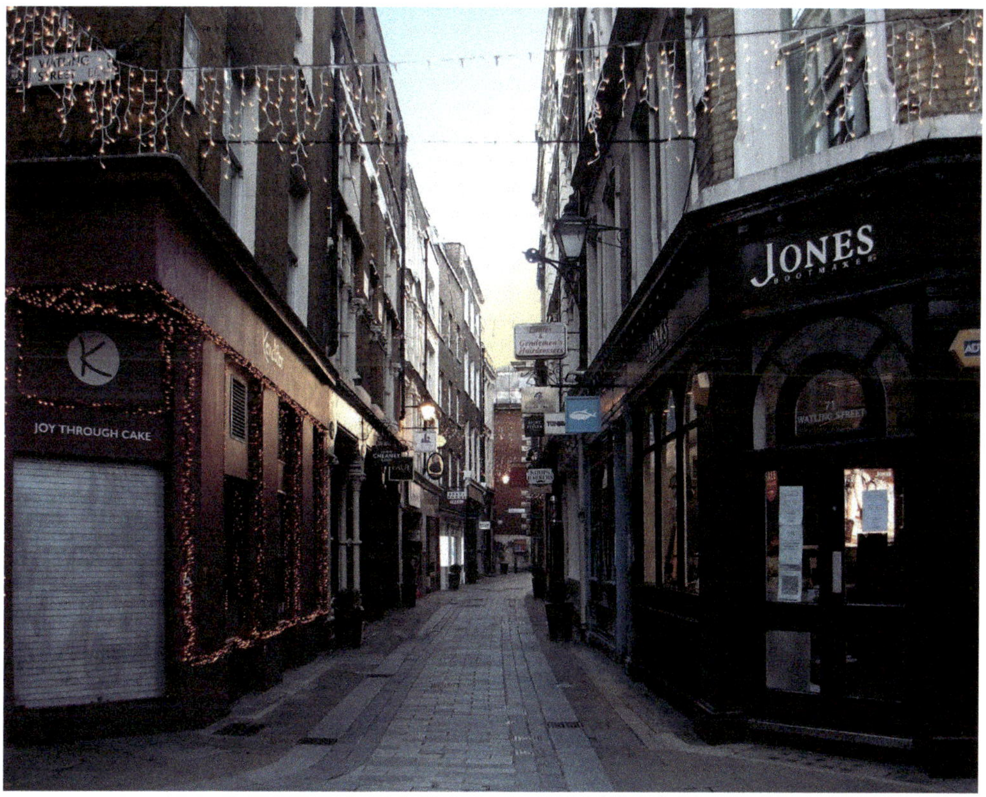

Bow Lane, EC4.

ground was used to bury London's plague victims. Since first built, Moorgate had been refurbished and enlarged before being severely damaged during the Great Fire. It was replaced by a stone-built gate in 1672.

By this time city gates had lost their main defensive function and, along with other London gates, Moorgate was taken down in 1762, the stonework used to repair the starlings (bulwarks surrounding bridge supports) of the widened centre arch of London Bridge. The street, known as Moorgate, was laid out during the mid-1800s and ran from the Bank of England, across the thoroughfare of London Wall, where the old gate once stood, and north towards Islington. The area around the street, also referred to as Moorgate, became the centre of insurance and banking. English poet John Keats was born in the Swan and Hoop Inn on Moorgate, now named Keats at The Globe, situated close to the original site of Bethlem Hospital, also known as Bedlam, a facility that specialised in the care and control of psychiatric patients.

The London Wall was a defensive structure that surrounded Roman Londinium. This name is preserved in a road running along part of the northern boundary between Aldersgate Street and Wormwood Street, which itself takes its name from the wormwood that grew on the wall. Part of the old wall can be found in St Alfege Garden, and below the west end of London Wall are the remains of the west gate, the entrance to the Roman fort at Cripplegate.

After being heavily bombed during the Second World War, the whole length of London Wall has been rebuilt, with high office blocks each side, the Barbican estate to the north, and the Museum of London located above the road island junction to the western end of the road.

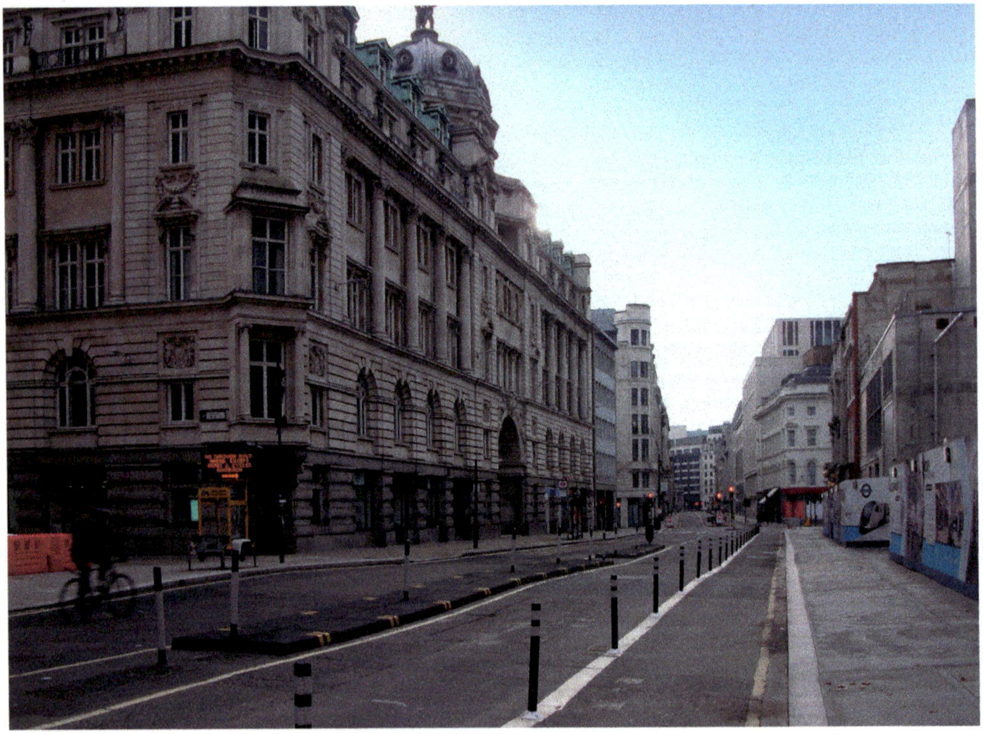

Moorgate, EC2.

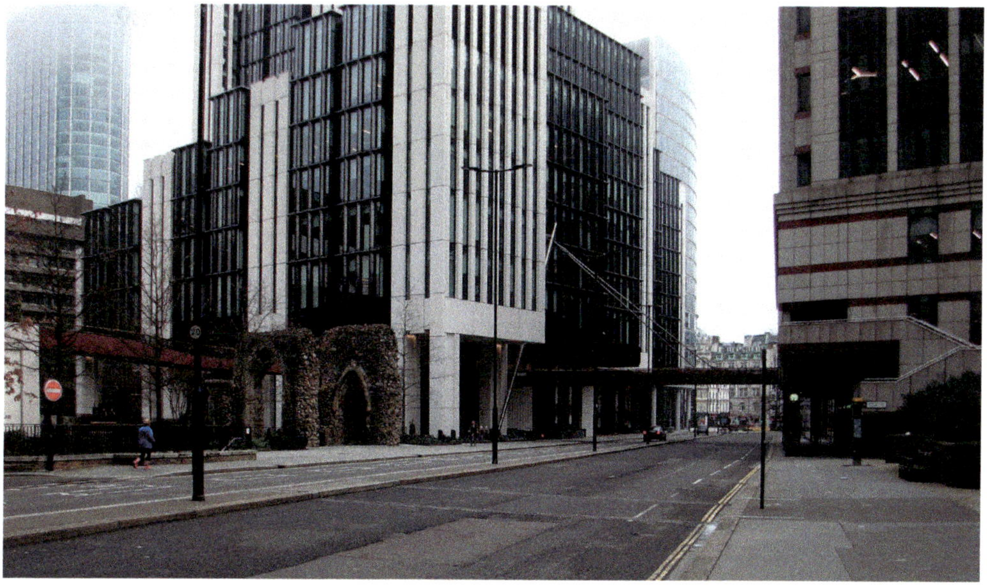

London Wall, EC2.

The Museum of London (opened in 1975) is an amalgamation of the London Museum and Guildhall Museum. The exhibits are a record of London's story from prehistoric times, through periods of adversity, the plague, fire and two world wars, through to modern times. I wonder if in the future it will also include the story of the Covid-19 pandemic – London's worst catastrophe in generations.

From the London Wall the Great Fire spread west, engulfing buildings down to the river, including London's great landmark St Paul's Cathedral, built by mason William Ramsey in 1332, the fourth erected on the site. The cathedral was so badly damaged it was impossible to restore and what remained was demolished, so plans were made to rebuild St Paul's.

Sir Christopher Wren submitted several designs to Charles II before the final plan was accepted, and when the royal warrant was issued to rebuild the cathedral, Wren was given liberty to make variations to the design. After works commenced, Wren dispensed with the planned tall steeple in favour of a large dome.

The outer dome was clad in lead on a timber framework, with an inner lower suspended dome erected below a brick-built conical structure supporting the timber beams and weight of the lantern above. On completion St Paul's Cathedral was the tallest building in the city.

Although several bombs struck the cathedral during the Second World War, only minor damage was caused, Prime Minister Winston Churchill issuing orders to London's firefighters to protect St Paul's from destruction at all costs. During one of the largest raids over London, a first wave of bombers dropped thousands of incendiary bombs on the city, designed to cause catastrophic infernos within the buildings, several of which landed upon Wren's architectural masterpiece but they were extinguished before fire took hold.

One, however, that hit the dome and struck fast, began burning through the leadwork in a bright green glow, giving the appearance to many onlookers across the city that St Paul's was ablaze. The device would have undoubtably ignited the timber structure within the dome if

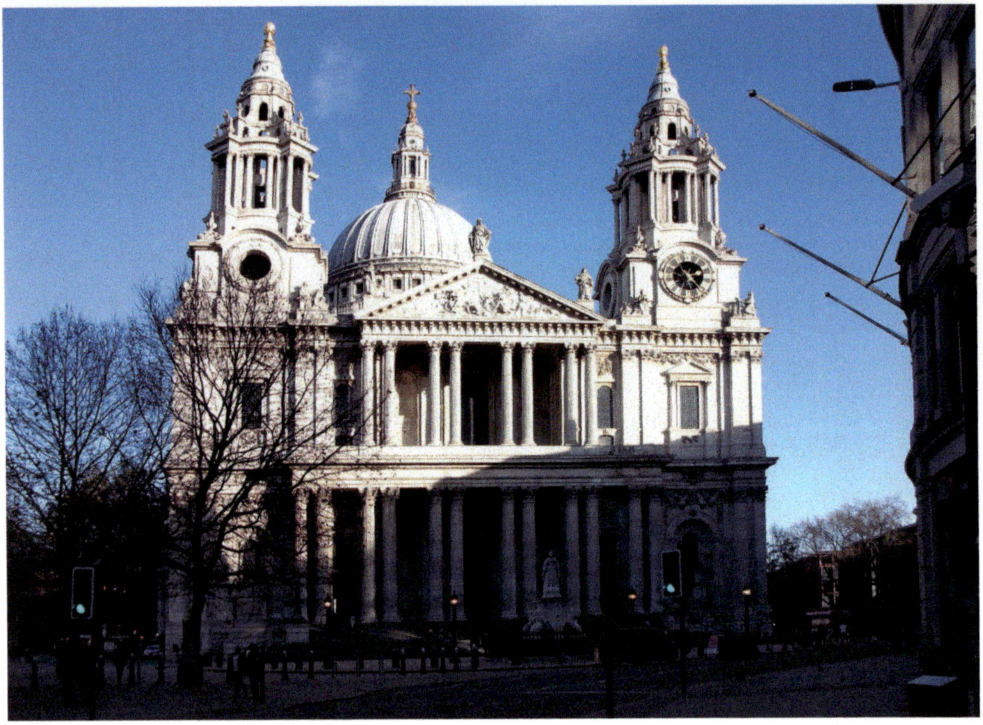

St Paul's Catherdral, EC4.

it had not suddenly fallen and was put out by the cathedral's fire wardens. On the morning following the raid, the sight of St Paul's Cathedral still standing tall among the smouldering ruins of the city gave people hope that while the cathedral survived, so would they.

From St Paul's the Great Fire spread west, driven on by an eastern wind, neither the city wall or the River Fleet providing an effective firebreak. One observer wrote, 'It rushed like a torrent down Ludgate Hill, and by five o'clock, was advanced as high as Fleet Conduit.' The Ludgate, the furthest gate west on the city wall and leading to a Roman burial ground near Fleet Street, was believed to have been named after the seventh-century Welsh King Lud. Rebuilt several times before being damaged in the Great Fire, the gate was repaired and then demolished in the mid-1700s.

The statues of Elizabeth I, King Lud and his two sons that decorated the gate were repositioned outside St Dunstan's Church, Fleet Street. Ludgate Hill was one of London's three ancient hills, rising to 17.6 meters above sea level, and during the seventeenth century became a fashionable place to shop. Diarist John Evelyn lived at the Hawk and Pheasant tavern between 1658 and 1659, and notabilities such as John Boswell, Benjamin Franklin and Joseph Priestly frequented the London Coffee House on Ludgate Hill, where juries from the Old Bailey were accommodated overnight while deliberating over verdicts.

A majority of the buildings were knocked down in the late 1860s to build Ludgate Hill station, which, after closure in 1923, was demolished along with a railway bridge in the 1990s.

The Fleet was the name given to the river running parallel to the city wall, flowing down to the Thames from Hampstead. A bridge over the Fleet that was destroyed in the Great

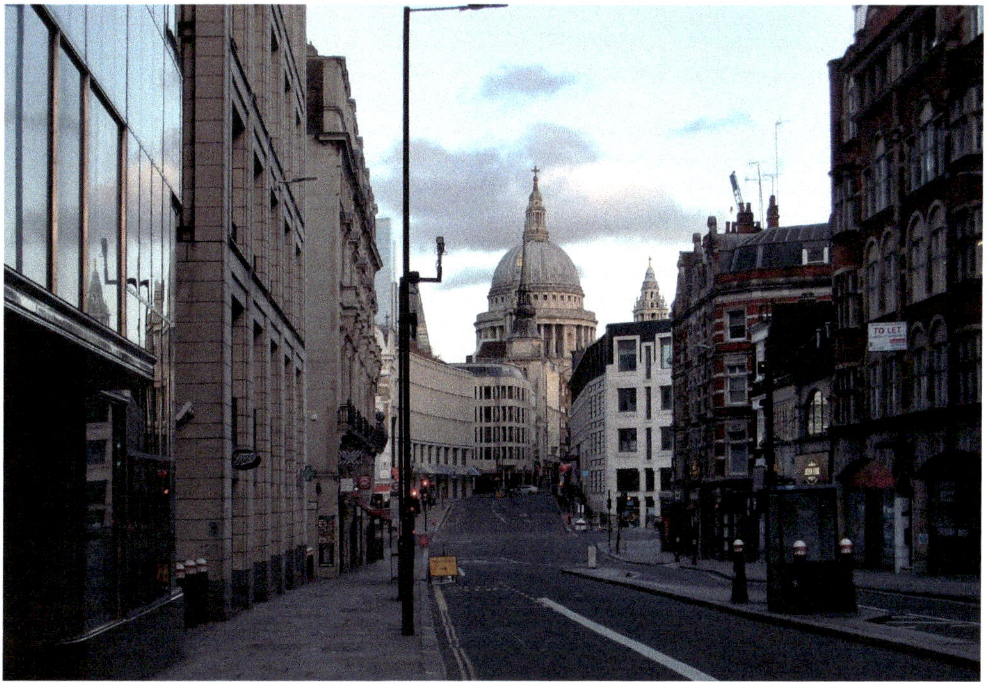

Ludgate Hill, EC4.

Fire was rebuilt and in use up until 1765, when it was removed for road widening. Used to transport goods, the Fleet became highly polluted from sewage, rubbish, and waste matter that was emptied into this once freshwater river by butchers and tanners, becoming commonly known as a plague-breeding sewer.

By the early 1800s the river had been channelled underground, bricked in, and covered over by roads and buildings. The properties to the east of Fleet Street, also destroyed in the fire, were rebuilt in a similar style. Noted as a place of publishing since the 1500s, London's first daily newspaper, the *Daily Courant*, was printed at Fleet Street in March 1702. A majority of the nation's weekly and Sunday papers were once published and printed at Fleet Street up until the end of the twentieth century, when the industry relocated to regenerated areas such as Wapping, Canary Wharf and Southwark.

One of London's earliest monthly periodicals, founded in 1733, *The Gentleman's Magazine*, published since 1781 at Red Lion Court, ran uninterrupted for almost 200 years. Named after the sixteenth-century Red Lion Tavern, which burned down during the Great Fire, the court was associated with the book trade, publishers, and printers.

The building towards the north end of the court was occupied up until the mid-1800s by printer, publisher and scholar Abraham Valpy, whose plaque can still be seen high up on the outer wall. The building Red Lion Chambers is now the chamber of barristers, specialising in criminal and terrorism law, appointed to act in cases such as the 2005 London bombings, which killed fifty-two people and injured hundreds more.

Fetter Lane, which runs from Fleet Street towards Holborn, was the furthest the Great Fire spread westwards. A place once frequented by beggars and idlers during the fourteenth

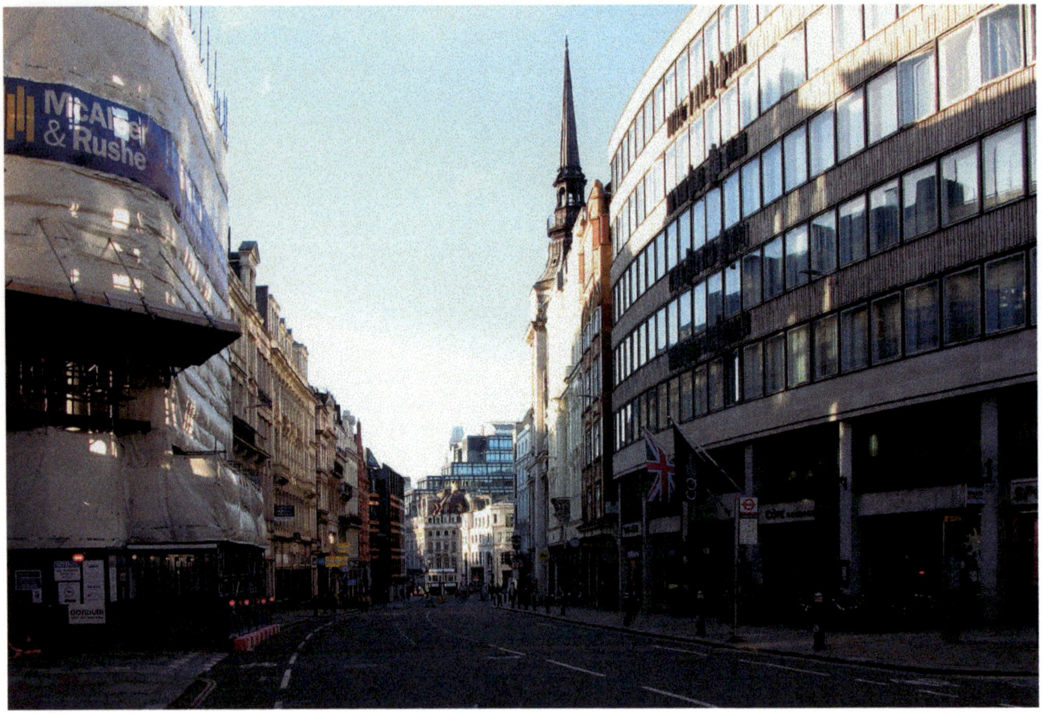

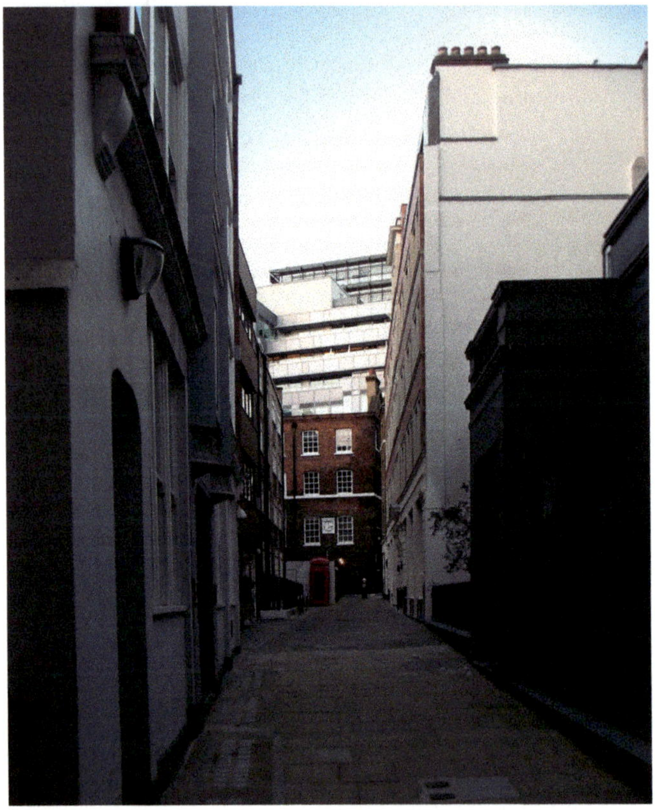

Above: Fleet Street, EC4.

Left: Red Lion Court, EC4.

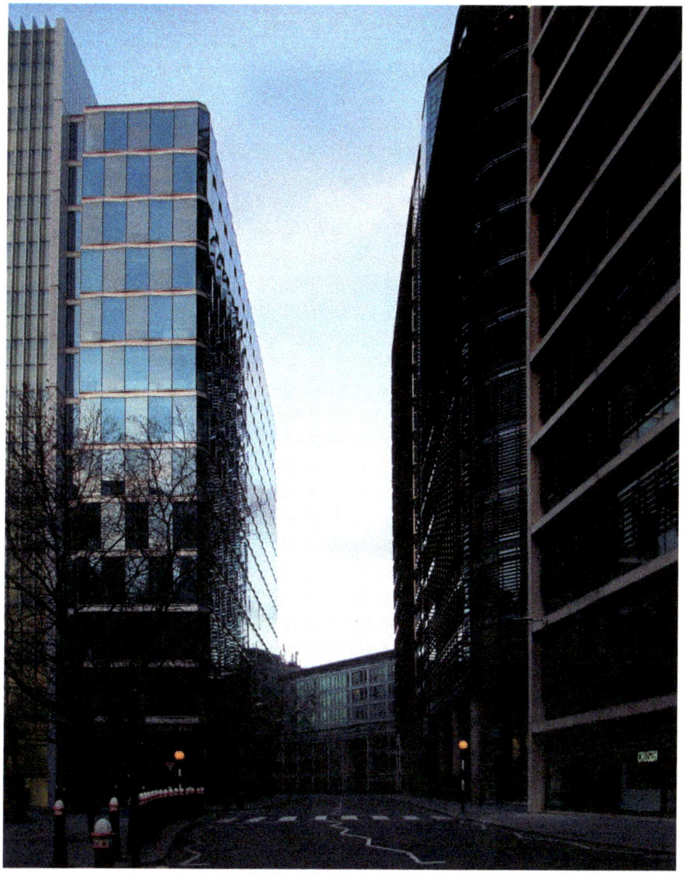

New Fetter Lane, EC4.

century, the name Fetter, formerly Faytor or Faiter, is derived from the Old French word *faitor*, a term used during the Middle Ages to describe a lawyer with a poor reputation. 'Fetter' also had associations with the Knights Templar: their armourers made protective lance vests, known as fetters, at the workshops on the lane.

In an attempt to control the Great Fire, Charles II and his brother James, Duke of York, took charge of the firefighting efforts. James created a series of fire posts around the city. One was set up at Fetter Lane and each was staffed by 130 men ready to take action as the fire approached. The buildings in the fire's path were either blown up or pulled down to make a firebreak.

Writer and diarist John Evelyn, who joined the fight against the fire, pulled down one of the last houses to make the firebreak and wrote, 'The stones of Paules flew like granados, the Lead mealting down the streetes in a streame, and the very pavements of them glowing with a fiery rednesse, so as nor horse nor man was able to tread on them.'

On the night of 4 September 1666, as the wind dropped then changed direction, the fire was blown south to the river, and the firefighters were able to gain control. Rebuilt after the fire, Fetter Lane suffered from heavy bombing during the Second World War, and many historic buildings were left in ruins. Remodelled after the war, Fetter Lane joined up with New Fetter Lane, an area that has gone through periods of modernisation and change, much like many areas within the old City of London.

3

Spread of the Plague

'The face of London was now indeed strangely altered.'

Daniel Defoe (1665)

As the city's population grew during the early seventeenth century there was an overspill into surrounding parishes outside of the city wall. St Giles-in-the-Fields was the largest of London's overcrowded outer parishes, a poor and poverty-stricken suburb made up of narrow streets, dilapidated tenements, brothels, inns, and gin houses.

St Giles-in-the-Fields originated as a leper hospital and chapel, founded in 1101 by Queen Matilda, wife of Henry I, on marshland outside the city. Dedicated to St Giles, the hospital was closed by Henry VIII. A church erected at the site served the poor moving to the parish, vagrants expelled from the city, French and Irish refugees, and dismissed black servants (known as St Giles Blackbirds), who were all forced onto the streets to beg. Although a wealthy parish, the tenements built on the marsh suffered from the damp and became increasingly overcrowded, and the unhealthy and the unsanitary conditions people were forced to live under became a great cause of concern.

In December 1664, the first of London's victims of the Great Plague fell ill and died in the parish at the north end of Drury Lane. Although by the cold winter months the epidemic had subsided, by the following May the plague, like today's Covid virus, had mutated to infect people at a furious pace and spread throughout the parish and into adjoining districts. By the end of the year thousands who died were buried in the churchyard of St Giles.

The south of the parish of St Giles was made up mostly of wasteland known as Cock Pye Fields, which property developer Thomas Neale acquired after the Great Fire with the intension of creating a fashionable residential district Seven Dials. The seven streets were laid out in a star with a Doric sundial pillar at the centre, the arrangement creating triangular plots to maximise the length of properties rented out per foot on the frontage rather than per square foot inside.

Through the following century, thieves and vagabonds were drawn to Seven Dials, which at one time had a tavern on the corner of each block. When the central sundial pillar was

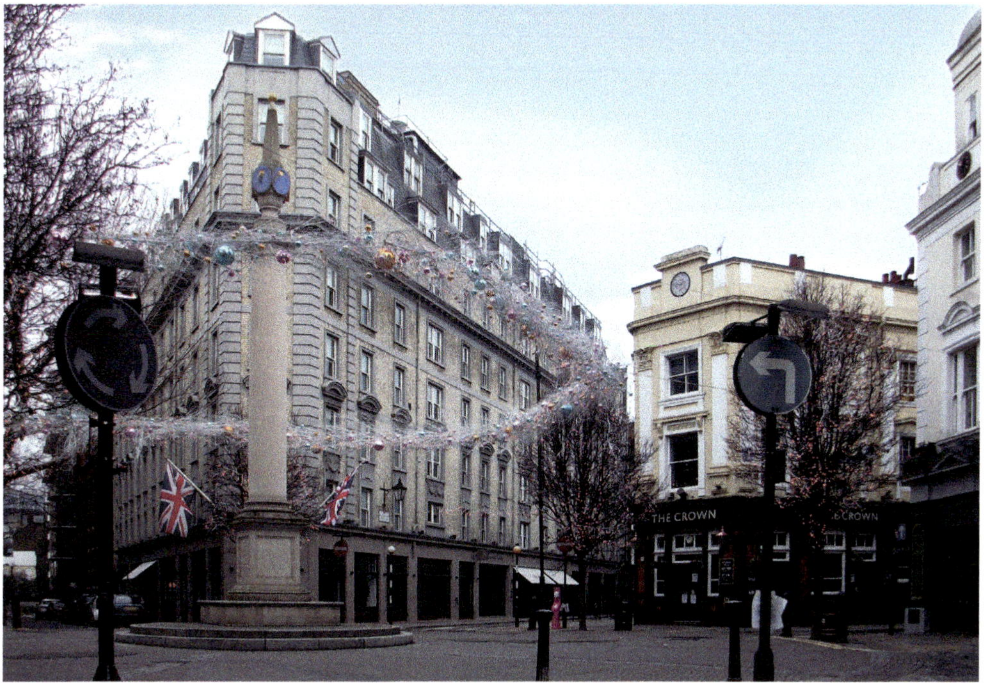

Seven Dials, WC2.

removed in 1773 (later re-erected on a green at Weybridge), a rumour spread that a mob tore it down searching for money believed buried at its base.

During a major redevelopment of the area to create Charing Cross Road and Shaftesbury Avenue, all but two of the Seven Dials blocks were cleared and rebuilt. In 1989, a copy of the original pillar was erected back at the centre of Seven Dials, now a fashionable district of London as Neale had first intended. Usually busy with shoppers, sightseers, and theatregoers, the streets of Seven Dials have been comparatively empty throughout lockdown.

To the west of Seven Dials, King Street and King's Head Court were renamed Neal's Yard and Neal's Yard Court in the mid-1800s in recognition of the role Thomas Neale played in cleaning up London's gambling dens. Along with property development, Thomas Neale acted as groom to Charles II, James II, and William III, tasked with organising royal gambling events. Charles II also assigned Neale to take charge of London's gambling and close down all illegal gambling houses, a majority located in the rundown areas of the city.

The gambling dens frequented by the poor were known as 'lower hells' and those that were visited by the rich were 'hells'. In the hope of increasing what little money they had, the poor could lose it all on a turn of a card; those successful would then often spend their winnings on gin and the prostitutes who hung around dens of immorality.

The Victorian properties on Neal Street were mostly independently run shops with accommodation above, and Neal Yard was made up of workshops and warehouses, both areas that have since become Covent Garden's trendiest places to shop and socialise. Over lockdown the specialist food and fashion shops, bars, cafés, and restaurants have had to close their doors to the public.

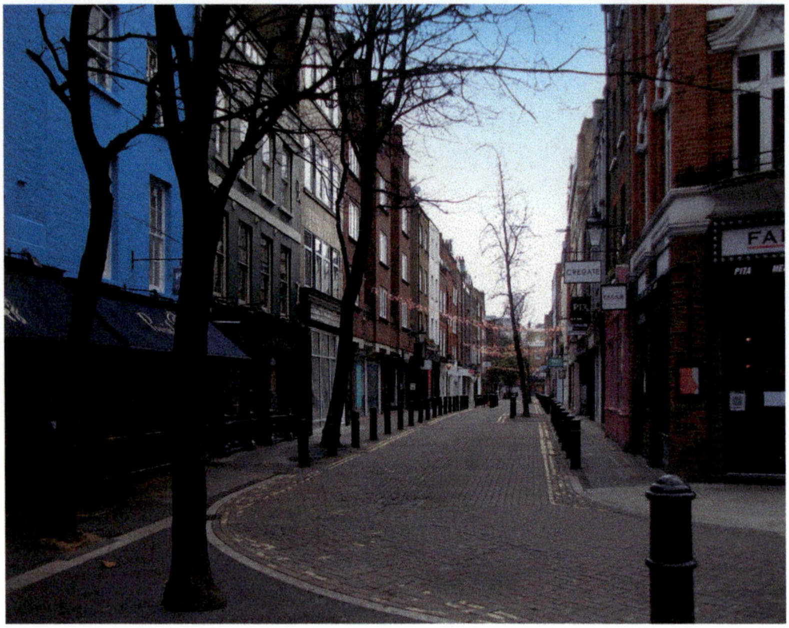

Left: Neal Street, WC2.

Below: Bow Street, WC2.

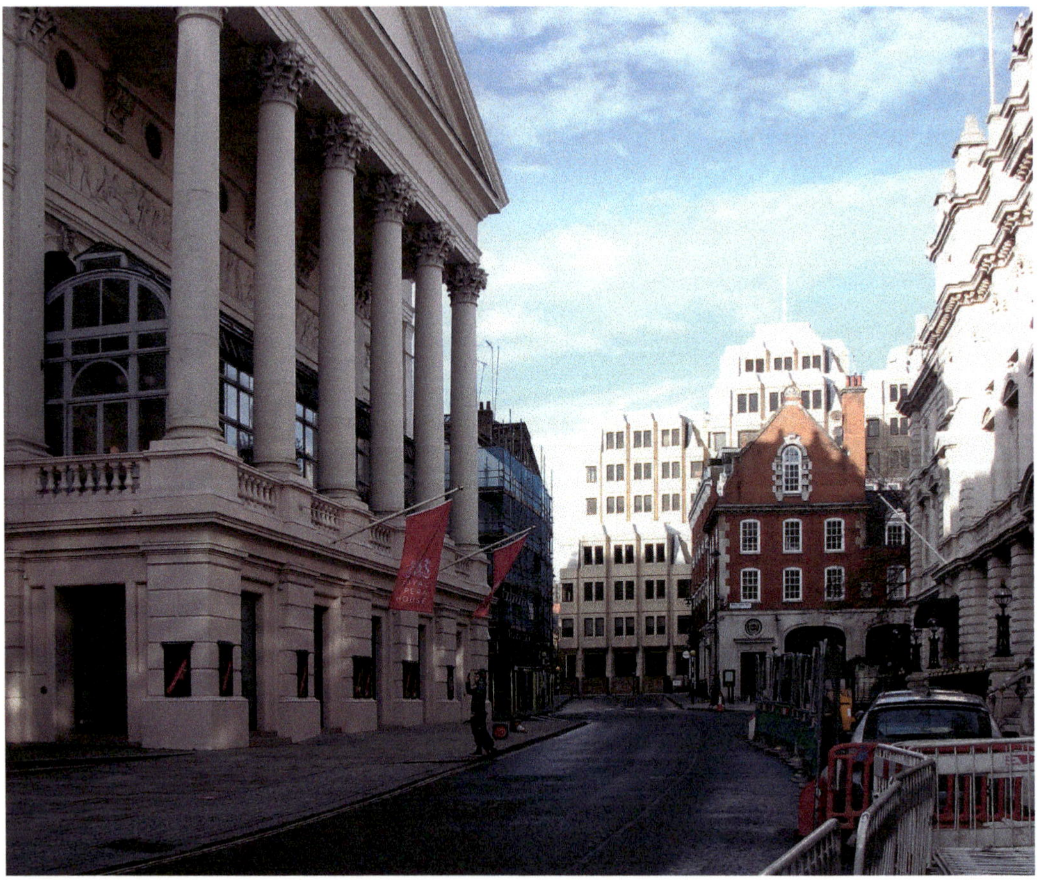

During days of the Great Plague London had no official police to enforce the restrictions introduced to attempt to control its spread. At the outbreak of 1630s plague, London's Privy Council had ordered the infected to be shut in their homes, a watchman placed outside to stand guard. London's watchmen would later work alongside volunteers known as 'thief takers' to keep law and order.

It was founded in the mid-1700s by a resident of Bow Street: writer and magistrate Henry Fielding. This voluntary force, based at Bow Street Magistrates' Court, later became known as Bow Street Runners, earning an income from securing convictions at the court. Bow Street magistrates' court was erected in 1703, some sixty years after the street was developed for residential use. Following on from Bow Street Runners, the Metropolitan Police, founded in 1829 by Robert Peel, operated a station house from 1832 at Bow Street, which led to the construction of a new magistrates' court, completed by 1881.

The Royal Opera House, opposite the court, is the third theatre to occupy the site – the previous two were destroyed by fire. A wild and raucous place at night, after the theatre first opened the gentrified residents began moving out as the district became just as well known for prostitution and pornography as it was for operatic performances.

Running to the rear of the Royal Opera House, Hart Street, renamed Floral Street in 1895 to reflect its closeness to Covent Garden flower and vegetable market, was a notorious thoroughfare where many inns and taverns doubled as brothels. During the 1700s, Hart Street became a popular haunt of the gay community. A pillory erected in the street was used to punish, as well as humiliate, those partaking in sexual acts seen as unacceptable to London society at the time.

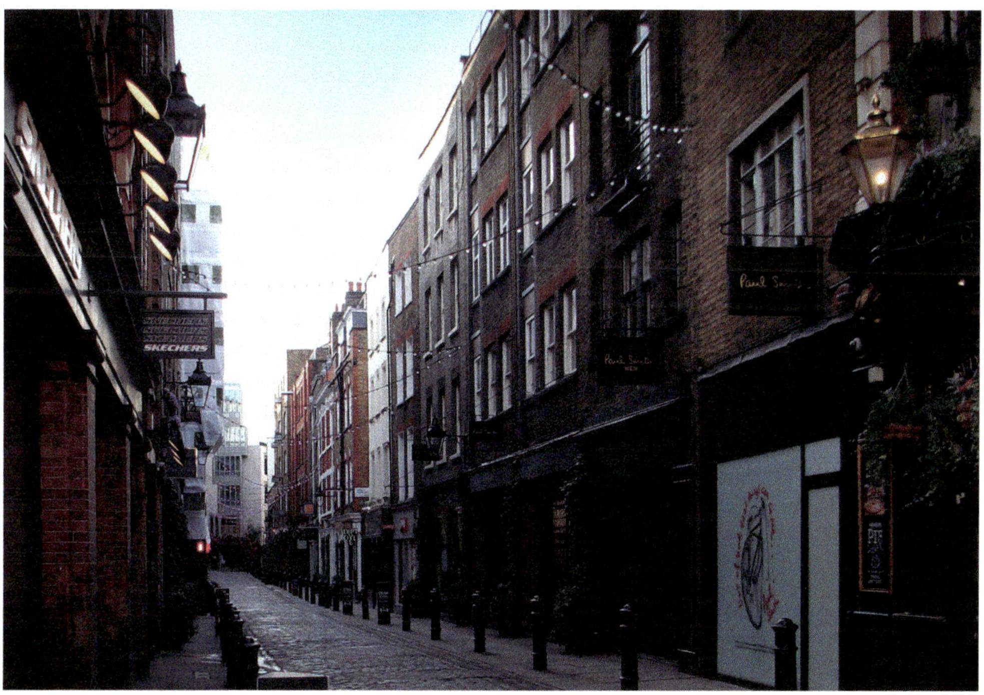

Floral Street, WC2.

On leaving the theatre at the end of an evening's performance, male members of the audience of a certain persuasion would make their way out onto Hart Street – London's first red light district. By the early 1800s, the area consisted of dark, narrow passages and secluded alleyways, inhabited by a poor and bad class of people, gaining the reputation as place where syphilis and cholera was rampant.

Although associated with the acting fraternity, Drury Lane, which took its name from Drury House, an Elizabethan mansion built by Sir Thomas Drury, was also notorious for its gin houses and 'pagnios' brothels. Before demolished in the early 1800s, the mansion was converted into a tavern after the gardens and courtyard were built upon.

Between the sixteenth and seventeenth centuries, Drury Lane was a fashionable place of residence, where two of the earliest female actors to perform on stage, Nell Gwynne and the Duchess of Bolton, Lavinia Fenton, resided.

In the early 1900s most of the district was cleared to make way for the development of Aldwych and Kingsway. When the street was widened the Prince of Wales public house, rebuilt at the base of offices adjacent to Freemasons Hall, was named after the future king, George VI, Grand Master of Freemasons.

Before the Great Plague London suffered from a series of plague epidemics, which started with the Black Death. In 1636, London's Privy Council reported plague in four parishes outside the city wall and quarantined houses on St Martin's Lane and Long Acre.

St Martin Lane was built in 1610 on acreage granted to the Earl of Salisbury, the properties a mixture of large houses with coach houses and stables, and tradesmen's

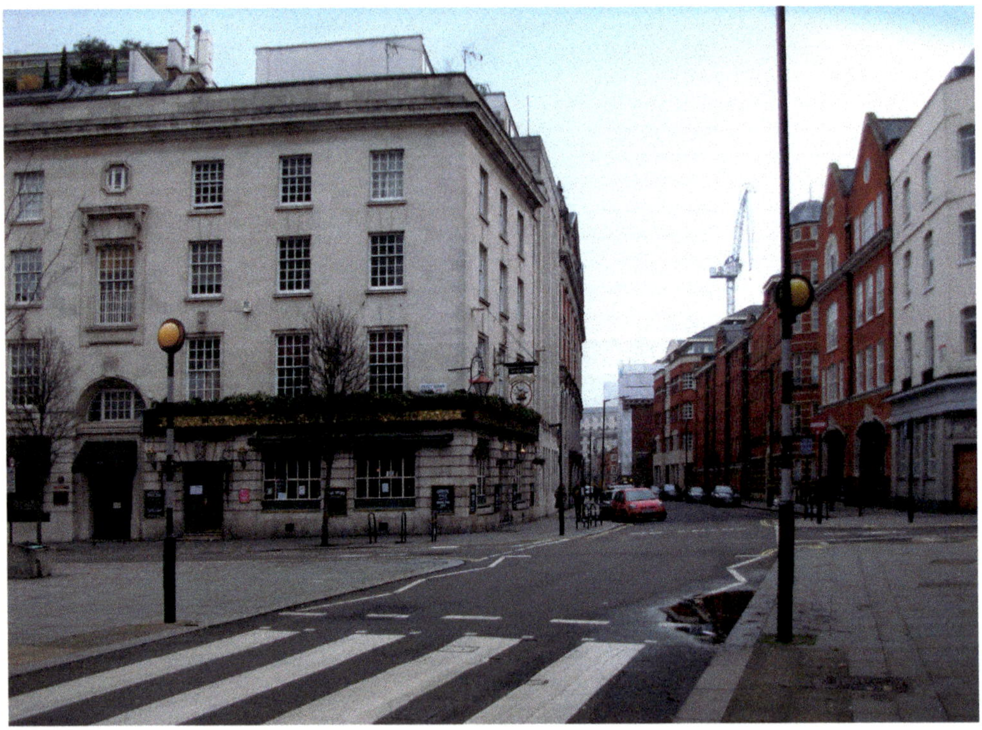

Drury Lane, WC2.

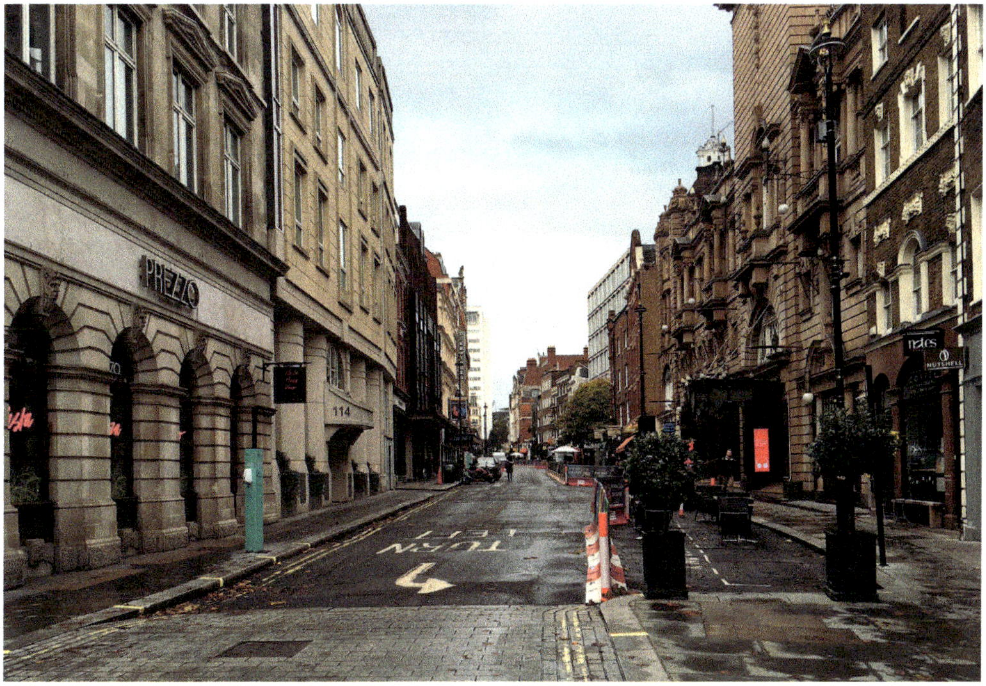

St Martin's Lane, WC2.

workshops. From the eighteenth century onwards St Martin's Lane grew into a fashionable area of art and entertainment, consisting of an art academy, music publishers, inns, a coffee house, and theatres, including the London Coliseum (opened in 1904), one of London's most luxurious variety theatres.

Edward VI granted Long Acre, once a narrow strip of land used as a market garden, to John Russel, 1st Earl of Bedford, in 1552, whose descendants acquired a licence to build houses on the land and to the south at Covent Garden Square.

The 4th Earl of Bedford secured the services of the king's Surveyor of Works, Inigo Jones, to design and build a new square with tall, elegant, terraced properties on three sides and a church, St Paul's, on the western side, the houses leased to London's well-to-do. By 1665, at the beginning of the Great Plague, the rich and poor coexisted at Covent Garden, with the wealthy occupying large houses surrounding the square and the destitute living in overcrowded unsanitary tenements.

As the market grew in size the rich of Covent Garden were soon relocating to the more fashionable districts to the west of London, and many of their houses were converted into lodgings, while others became brothels. By the late 1800s new properties had replaced the seedier establishments and the flower and vegetable market, although no longer adequate for the needs of the trade it continued to operate in Covent Garden until relocating to Nine Elms in 1974.

Established in 1656, nine years before the Great Plague, London's most well-known fruit and vegetable market began as a few temporary stalls in the garden of the Earl of Bedford's house, adjacent to Henrietta Street, named after Henrietta Maria, the wife of Charles I.

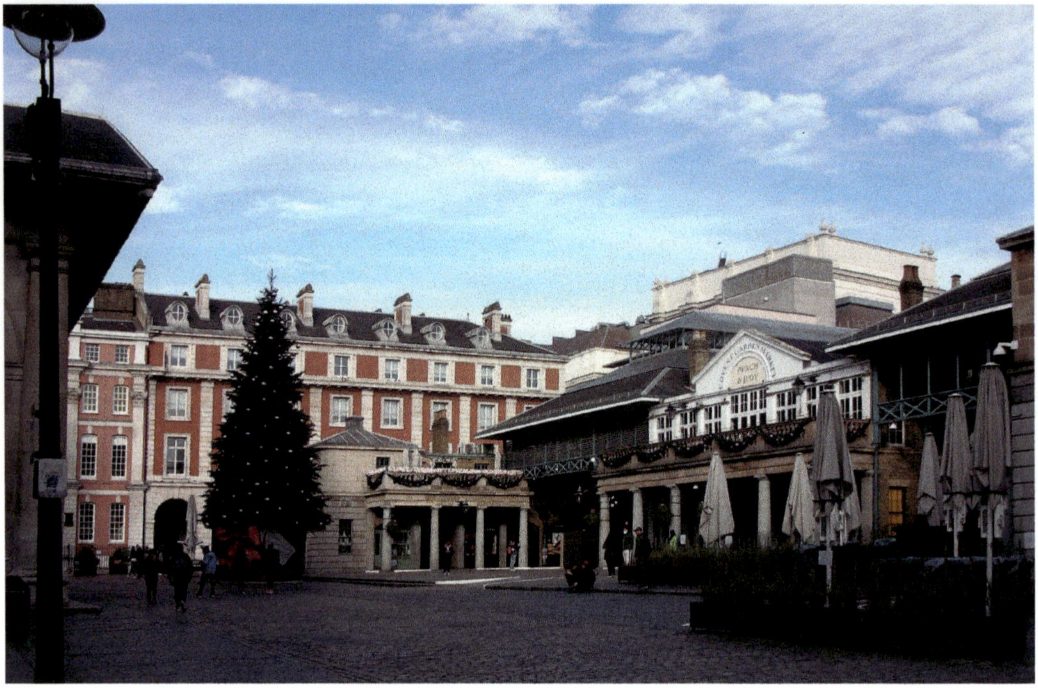

Covent Garden, WC2.

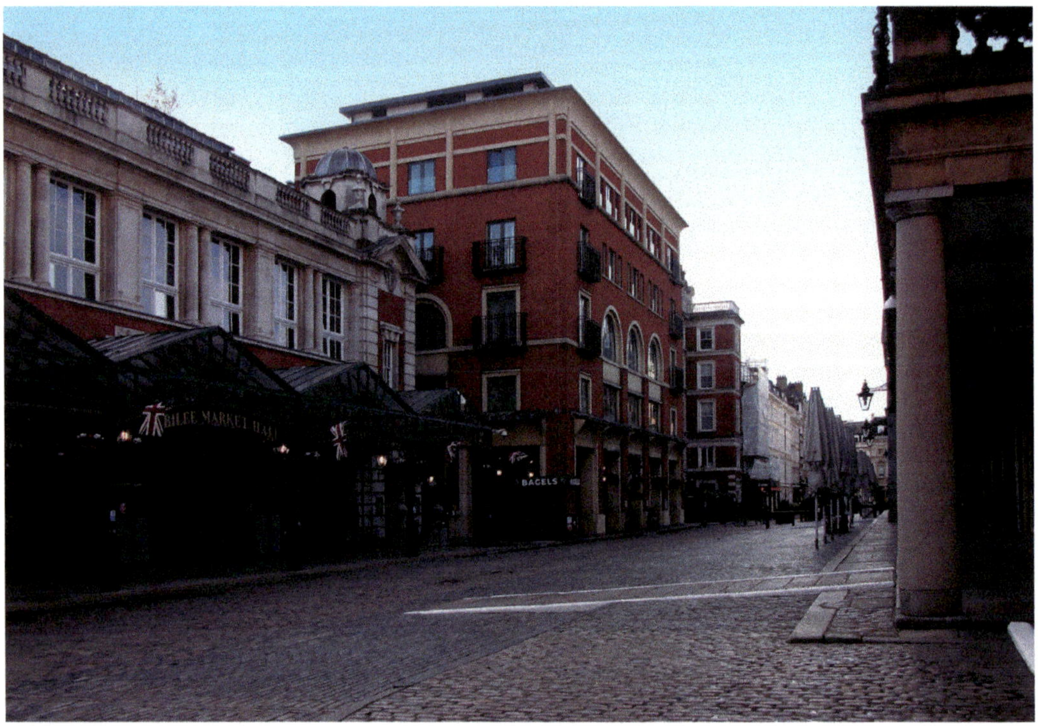

Henrietta Street, WC2.

Granted a licence by Charles II to hold a market every day except Sundays and Christmas Day, the lease was sold in 1678 and permanent market shops buying and selling fruit, herbs, roots and flowers were erected against the garden wall of the earl's house.

During one of the earliest plague outbreaks the authorities discouraged people from consuming uncooked fruit, believing it to be one way the disease was transmitted. They then banned its sale altogether.

Most cases of the plague were recorded in densely packed pockets where residents lived in squalid conditions, and although many streets around Covent Garden fitted this category, very few deaths were recorded. To the south, on the Strand, where bishops, noblemen and royal courtiers lived, there were even fewer recorded plague deaths. The Strand, lined with shops, theatres, cafés, restaurants, and public houses today, began as a bridlepath running adjacent to the Thames, a time before the embankment was created.

By the twelfth century several large mansions had been erected off the Strand, which had become the main route between the City of London and the Palace of Westminster. To the south of the Strand is one of London's most famous hotels, The Savoy, which was opened in 1889 and erected on land once occupied by Savoy Palace, a large thirteenth-century manor, the residence of Peter, Earl of Richmond, of the House of Savoy.

Many of the grand mansions were demolished during 1600; the Savoy Palace was destroyed previously during the Peasants' Revolt. By the eighteenth century the Strand had become noted for its coffee houses, chop houses and taverns, where there were more theatres than on any other London street. The alleyways off the Strand were once the haunt

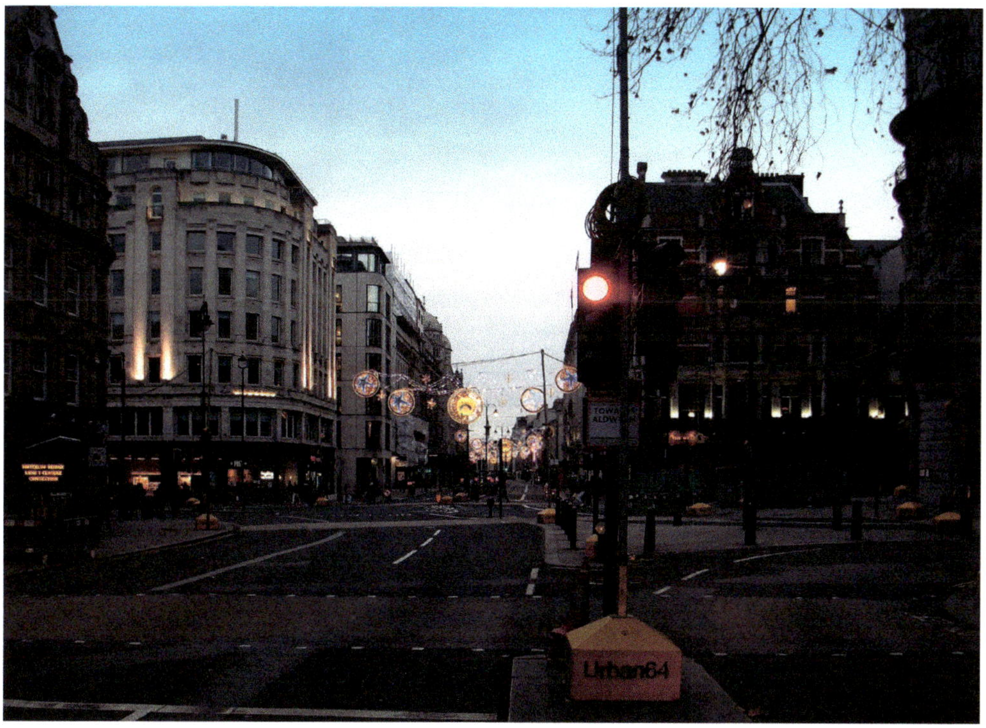

The Strand, WC2.

of prostitutes, pickpockets, and thieves, attracted by the wealthy theatregoers and travellers passing by.

Once the haunt of Tom Cox, known as the 'Handsome Highwayman' and hung at Tyburn in 1690, Essex Street was built at the site of another riverside mansion, Essex House, belonging to Robert Devereux, Earl of Essex. A favourite of Elizabeth I, after Essex attempted to lead a rebellion against the queen he retreated to the mansion with his men, surrendering when surrounded by the queen's men at arms. Found guilty for treason, Essex was executed at Tower Green.

Opposite the junction of Little Essex Street stands a public house, the Edger Wallace, dating to 1777. This was originally the Essex Head and was once home to the Essex Head Club, established by author, poet and playwright Samuel Johnson, and fellow of the Royal College of Physicians, Richard Brocklesby. The southern end of the street leads through an arch towards Middle Temple, one of the four Inns of Court entitled to call their members to the English Bar as barristers.

The Law Courts on the Strand, opened by Queen Victoria in 1882, were built to bring together all superior courts dealing with civil law. Until the reign of Henry II, royal justice had been administered wherever the king was in residence; the king then decreed judges should hear cases at specific places rather than travel with the royal court. The site chosen for the law court was an area consisting of some 450 slum properties on Butcher Row, occupied by around 4,000 of London's poor. It was purchased relatively cheaply and paid for out of public funds.

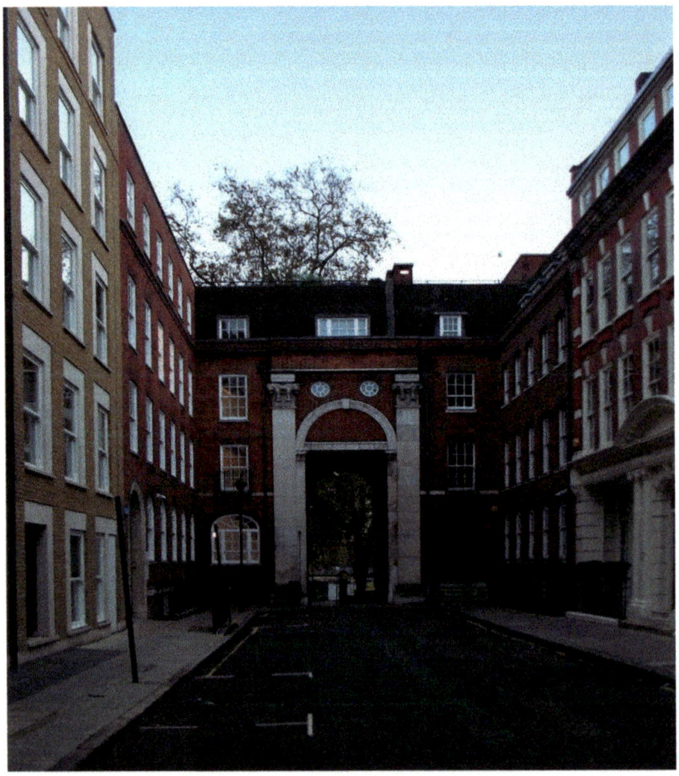

Essex Street, WC2.

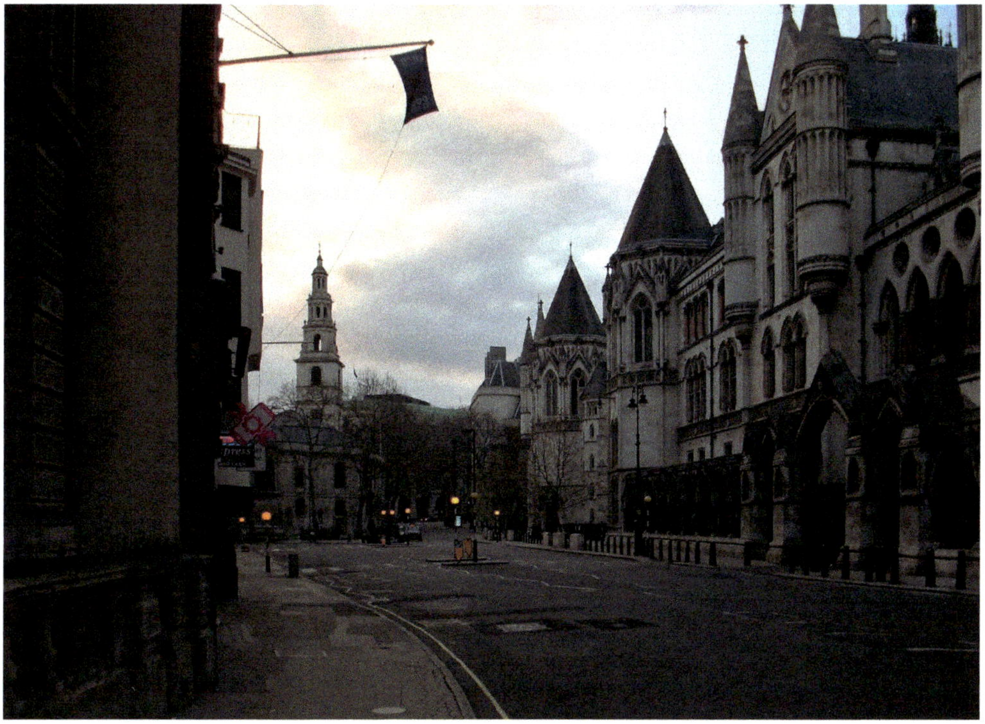

Royal Courts of Law, WC2.

On the night of 13 June 1915, during an air raid over London, a Zeppelin flying a course from the Strand to Aldwych, then onwards to Holborn and Whitechapel, dropped several bombs and incendiaries on its way. At least three incendiary bombs fell on the Royal Courts of Justice without causing serious damage.

One of the Zeppelin's explosive bombs, however, fell on Lincoln's Inn, badly damaging the stained-glass window of Lincoln's Inn Chapel. Designed by Inigo Jones, the chapel was built between 1620 and 1623 at the site of a smaller fifteenth-century chapel, then extensively rebuilt twice during the following two centuries. Adjacent to Lincoln's Inn and one of the four London Inns of Court, Lincoln's Inn Fields is the largest public square in London and was laid out in the mid-1600s. Before lockdown it would be crowded with people enjoying themselves away from the hustle and bustle of Kingsway and High Holborn.

Once used for grazing, the land belonged to St Giles Hospital and was leased before being seized by the crown during the mid-1500s. Several unsuccessful schemes were proposed to develop Lincoln Inn Fields before William Newton received permission to build thirty-two houses around the square after petitioning Charles I in the 1630s. Although Lincoln's Inn was a place where the wealthy lived, it was not safe from the plague, which arrived in the early summer of 1665. All the members of the Inns of Court were told to leave and those who had properties in the country fled London.

At the highest point in the City of London, High Holborn runs from Shaftesbury Avenue to the junction of Grays Inn Road. The timber-framed building of Staple Inn, situated

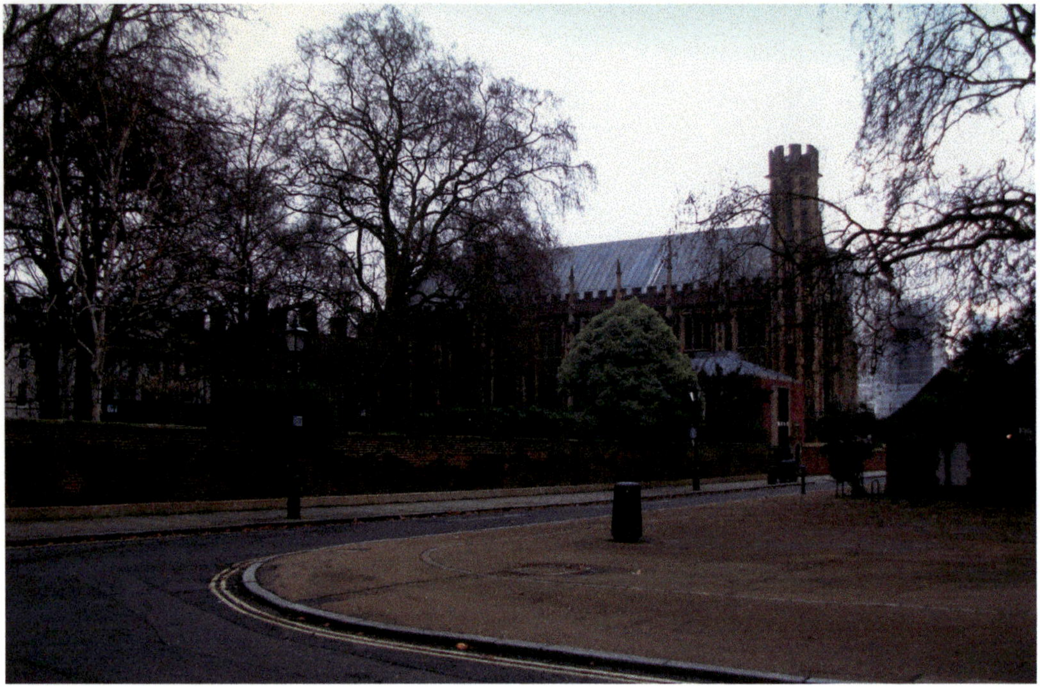

Lincoln Inn, WC2.

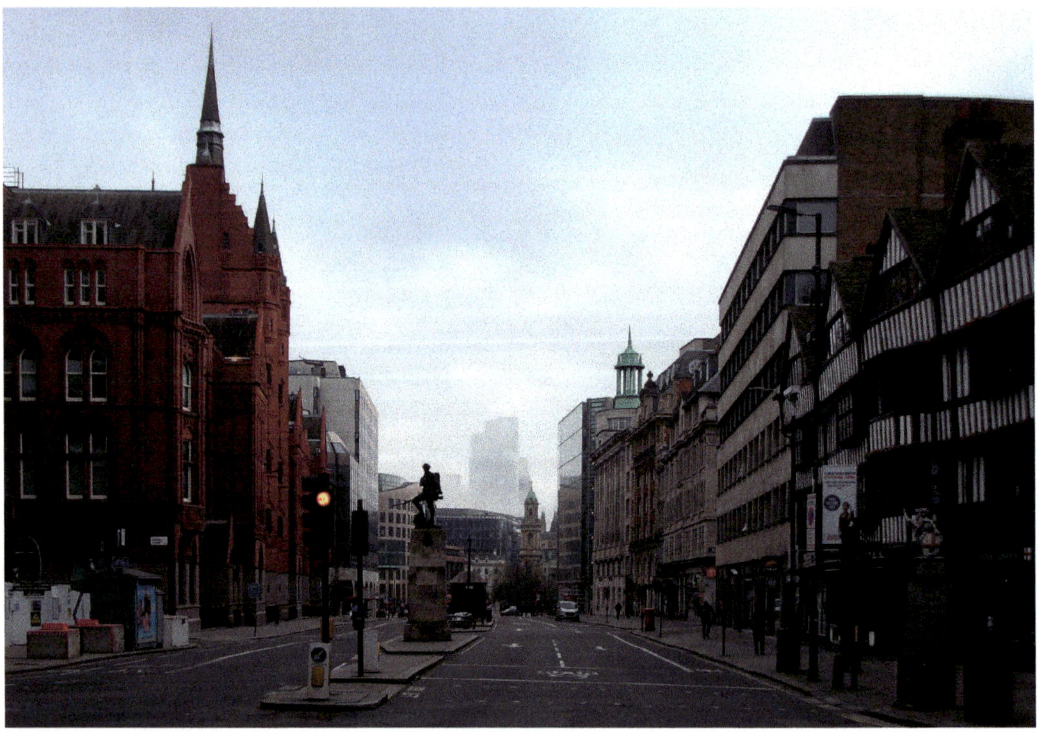

High Holborn, WC1.

adjacent to Chancery Lane Tube station entrance, is partly Elizabethan-built and is the only surviving Inn of Chancery – a collection of institutions attached to the Inns of Court.

Originally serving as a place where wool was weighed and taxed, Staple Inn was severely damaged by bombing in 1944, but was later fully restored.

The large, red, Victorian Gothic building opposite, known as Holborn Bars, was erected on the site of Furnival's Inn, a medieval building demolished and rebuilt as apartments in 1818, before being redeveloped as the Prudential Assurance headquarters in 1879.

At one time there were many taverns and places of sporting entertainment located on High Holborn. Many of these buildings, however, after being damaged from bombing during the Second World War, were later demolished and modern buildings erected in their place.

Chancery Lane was notable for its high number of lodgings for those in the legal profession, as well as the many taverns, coffee and eating houses that supplied the legal fraternity with plenty of food and drink. It was from one of these taverns, the Princes Arms on Chancery Lane, where *The Christians Refuge: Or Heavenly Antidotes Against the Plague* was sold by H. Marsh. This text contained spiritual remedies to combat the plague, medicinal recipes, and mortality statistics, and was just one of many plague information pamphlets and books published at the time. Originally known as New Street, the name changed to Chancellors Lane in 1377, after Edward II's Keeper of the Rolls of Chancery, and then Chancery Lane.

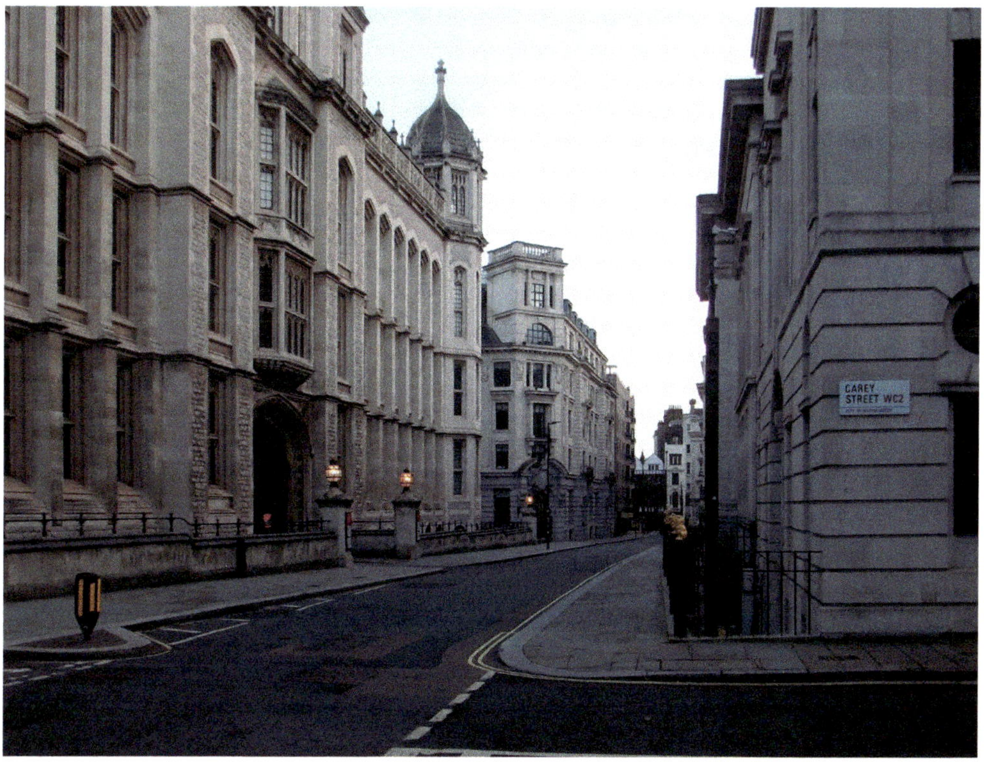

Chancery Lane, WC2.

Towards the north end are the London Silver Vaults, originating as Chancery Lane Safe Deposit Co. in 1885. To the southern end at the Strand is the main research facility of King's College London: the Maughan Library, named after an alumnus of the university.

The refurbished mid-nineteenth-century Gothic-style buildings, once occupied by the Public Records Office, were erected on the site of the Chapel of the Master of the Rolls, warden of Domus Conversorum, the House of Converts, established by Henry III in 1232, a residence provided to Jews converting to Christianity.

During the sixteenth century, a district from Holborn to Hatton Wall and between Leather Lane and Saffron Hill, was known as Hatton Garden. The main thoroughfare running to the right of a modern office block northwards from Holborn was named Hatton Street after Hatton House, residence of Elizabeth I's Chancellor, Sir Christopher Hatton. By the early 1700s, Hatton House had been demolished and a road and houses erected on the site, the street name changing to Hatton Garden.

Exclusively a place for London's gentry, up until the nineteenth century no shops were allowed on the upper part of the street. After jewellers working in silver and gold began occupying shops on the road during the mid-1800s, Hatton Garden became the busy centre of London's diamond trade.

Hatton Garden was heavily bombed during the Blitz. The building occupied by the Diamond Trading Company, the distribution branch of De Beers, was totally destroyed in an air raid. Today there are over 300 businesses and fifty shops dealing in precious metals and gemstones. It was believed the founder of De Beers, Charles Oppenheim, commissioned the statue of Albert, Price Consort, situated at Holborn Circus, but this has since been denied by De Beers.

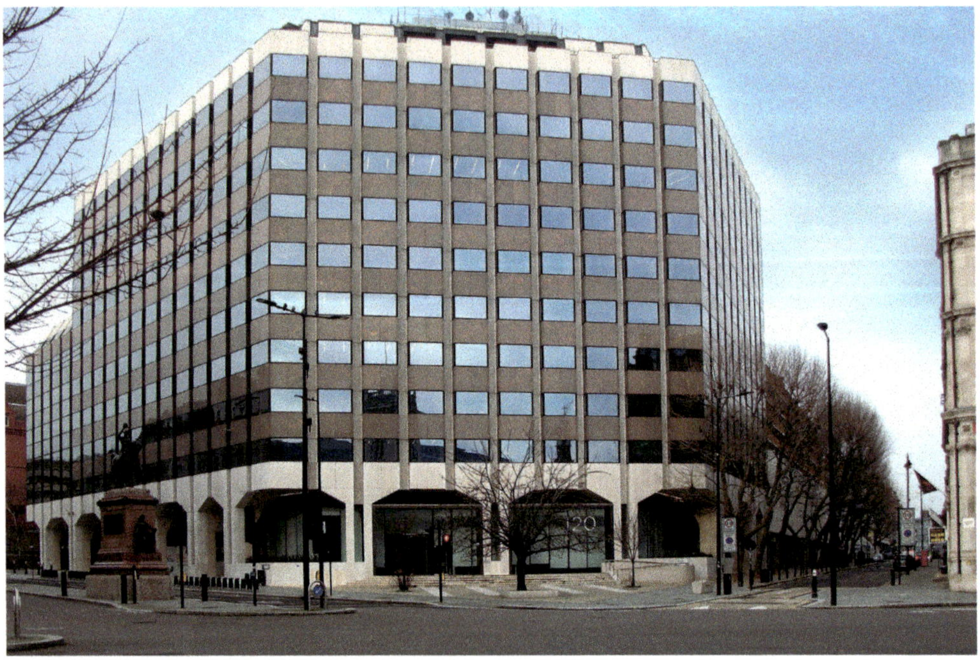

Hatton Garden, EC2.

Several robberies have taken place at Hatton Garden. In 1993 gems worth £7 million were stolen from Graff Diamonds and in 2015 burglars made off with valuables estimated to be worth £14 million from the Hatton Garden safe deposit facility. Although most of those involved in the robbery were later arrested, only a small amount of the stolen valuables was recovered.

When John of Gaunt's Savoy Palace was destroyed in 1381 by rioters blaming him for introducing the poll tax, he took up residence at Ely House, on Charterhouse Street, the London townhouse of the bishops of Ely. Henry VIII visited the house for five days of banqueting in 1531, the entourage consuming 100 sheep, fifty-one cows, twenty-four oxen, ninety-one pigs and hundreds of chickens and wildfowl.

The palace was used as a prison and hospital during the English Civil War and was under the ownership of Lord Hatton. Upon his death in 1772, the property, in much need of repair, reverted to the crown. All the properties apart from the Bishop's former chapel, St Etheldreda's Church, were demolished and tall brick-built terraced properties were erected on the site. At one time the police were not allowed to enter the private road through the gated entrance until invited.

On the north side of Smithfield, Charterhouse Street forms part of the old city boundary with Islington and Camden, the original offices of the Port of London Authority and several refrigerated warehouses, once used for storing meat, run parallel to the meat market. During the sixteenth century, this ancient street, then known as Charterhouse Lane, was just a narrow thoroughfare leading from Charterhouse Monastery gate to St John Street. After the expansion of the market the lane was incorporated into the new Charterhouse Street,

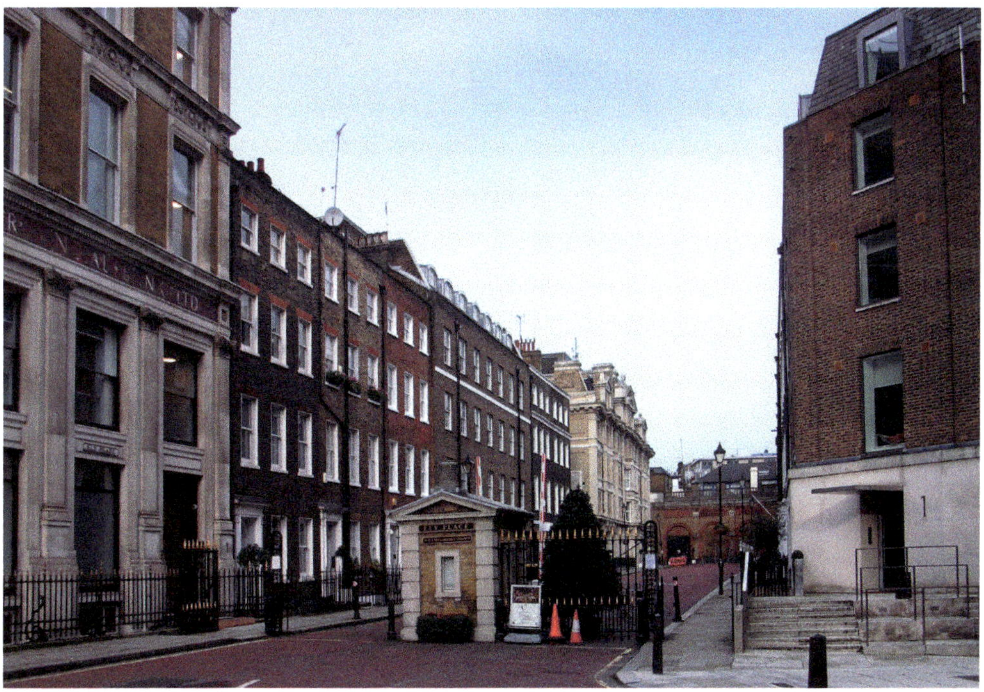

Ely Place, EC1.

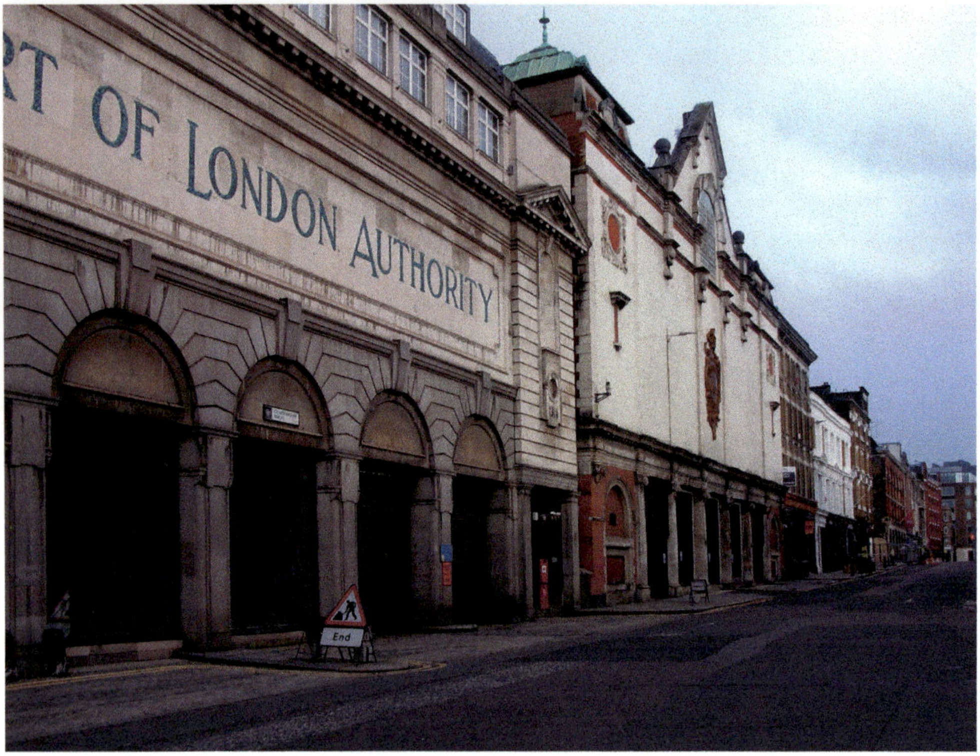

Charterhouse Street, EC1.

extending south-west to Holborn Circus. Charterhouse Street has become famed for its public houses and eateries, frequented before lockdown by market traders and city workers.

From Charterhouse Street, the course of the ancient River Fleet flows southwards, and can still be heard through a grating on the Smithfield side of the junction with Farringdon Road. Named after thirteenth-century goldsmith William de Farringdone, Farringdon Road was built over the River Fleet in 1737.

Spanning the Fleet Valley, the decorative Holborn Viaduct, erected between 1863 and 1869 to ease traffic flow into the city from the west of London, was built at a cost of £2.5 million – equivalent to around £250 million today. The four bronze statues erected on the bridge represent Commerce and Agriculture on the north side, and Science and Fine Arts on the south.

The world's first coal-powered electric power station was built at No. 57 Holborn Viaduct by the Edison Electric Light Company, supplying street lighting from Holborn Circus to St Martin's Le Grand, Newgate. The electric cables had to be laid in culverts on the viaduct as the company did not have permission to dig down into the street.

The Fleet Market, located north of Fleet Prison and consisting of two rows of shops, selling meat and vegetables, was cleared in the early 1800s to make way for the building of Farringdon Road. When the new Farringdon fruit and vegetable market proved to be unsuccessful, it was moved to a hall at nearby Smithfield meat market. Meat had been traded at Smithfield since the ninth century, making it one of the oldest markets in London.

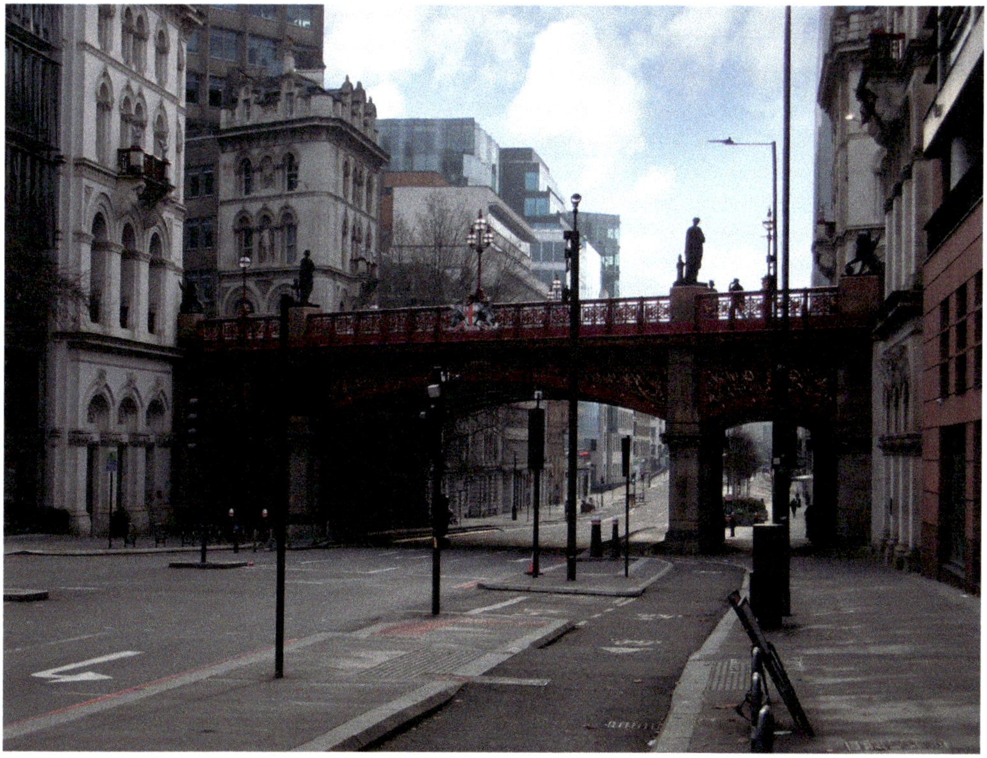

Farringdon Road, EC4.

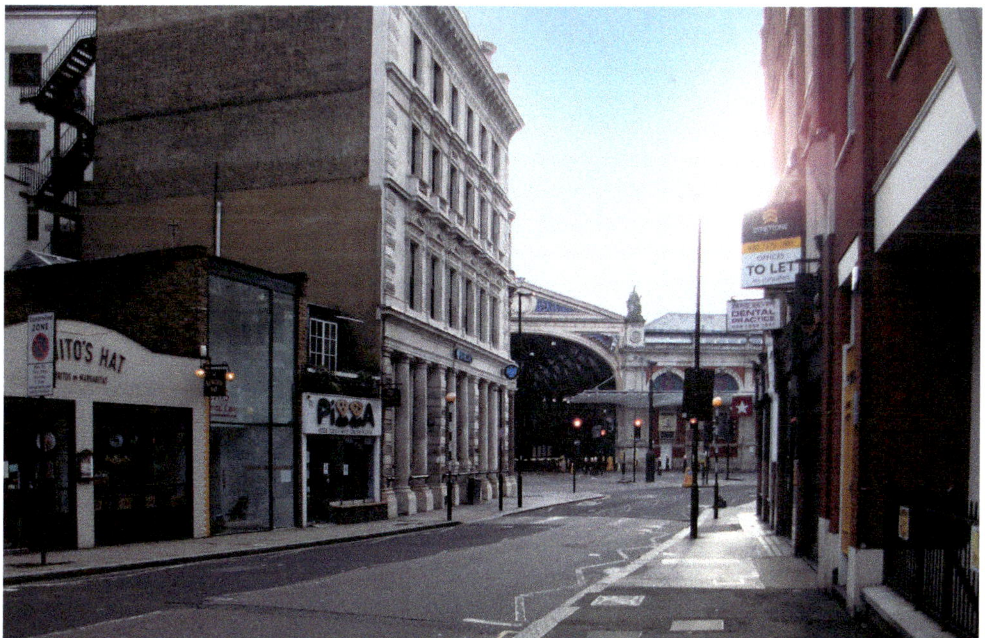

St John Street, EC1.

Opposite Smithfield, St John Street was an ancient route used by drovers and traders travelling from the north to the sale grounds and markets on the edge of the city. By the seventeenth century, with its many inns, brewhouses, stables and barns, St John Street evolved into a staging post for coaches.

Originally known as Smoothfield due to being a large plain of grass outside the city wall, Smithfield was well known as a place for horse trading during the Middle Ages, and afterwards for buying and selling pigs and sheep. After livestock trading moved to Islington in the mid-1800s, a market hall built by Henry Jones to a design based on the Crystal Palace was opened in 1868 as the London Central Meat Market. At Pye Corner, to the south of the market, a statue of a gold cherub mounted on the corner of an office block marks the spot where the Great Fire came to its end. Known as the Golden Boy, it was originally built into the front of the Fortune of War inn, which was demolished in 1910.

To the north of London Wall, Sir Walter de Manny, a knight of Edward III, gifted land to the city for use as a burial ground for victims of the Black Death, and in 1370 founded a Carthusian monastery at the site. During the reign of Henry VII the Carthusian priors were arrested for treachery after questioning the king's supremacy as head of the Church. After being tried and found guilty they were hung and quartered at Tyburn. Persecution of the monks continued until the monastery was surrendered to the king in 1537.

Transformed into a Tudor mansion, where Elizabeth I stayed prior to her coronation in 1558, by the early seventeenth century Charterhouse had become a school for boys and an almshouse founded by the richest commoner in England, Thomas Sutton.

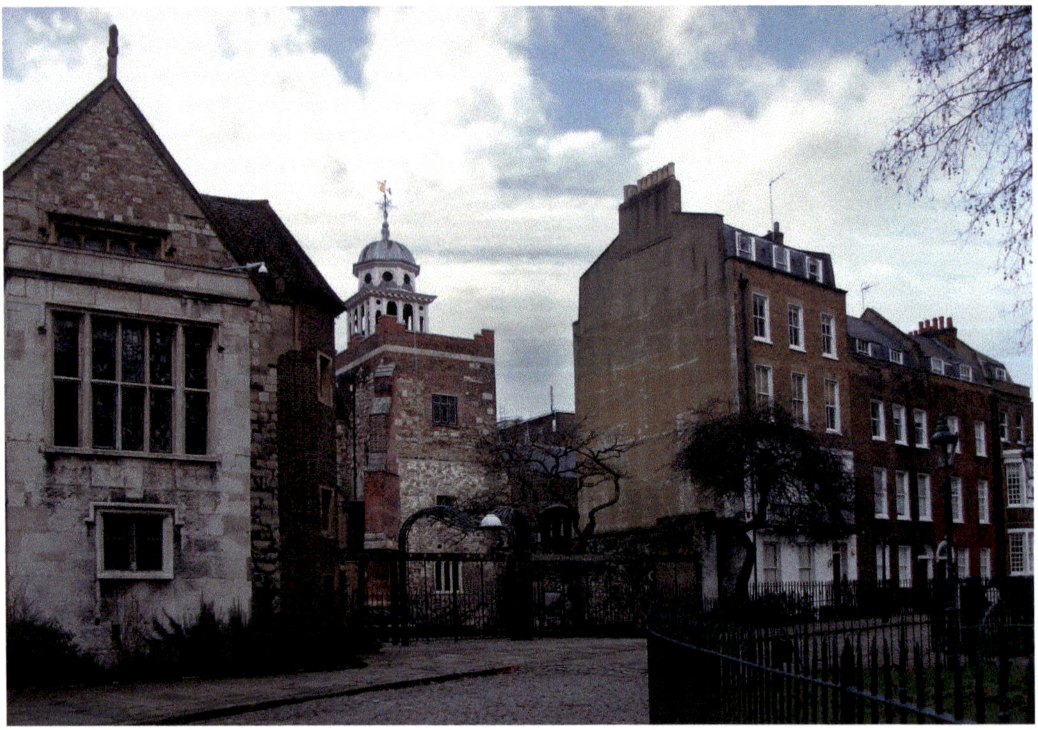

Charter House, EC1.

Although most of the older buildings were destroyed in a Second World War air raid, after restoration Charterhouse almshouse is now a museum and home to a community of elderly residents. During the building of the Crossrail link in 2013, one of London's largest burial pits was discovered at nearby Charterhouse Square, believed to hold hundreds of plague victims.

The main route out of London to Smithfield, Aldersgate Street, was named after the city gate that was damaged during the Great Fire. When the fire destroyed the Bishop of London's residence at St Paul's, his household relocated to Petre House on Aldersgate Street, where it is also claimed William Shakespeare once owned a property, located at the site of Barbican station.

The Barbican Estate, a huge Grade II listed residential complex consisting of tall towers and blocks adjacent to the Barbican Arts Centre and Museum of London to the south, was erected on the site where many historic buildings were destroyed by bombing during the Second World War. The only surviving historical landmark, Ironmongers Hall, is hidden within a complex of concrete walkways leading to the Barbican Centre. In Latin, *barbecana* was a term used to describe a defensive, fortified gate. The Barbican Centre was named after the Roman gated watchtower built into the London Wall.

As the plague spread out across London, the dead were swiftly buried in local church cemeteries, but as the death toll rose and the graveyards became full, dedicated pits were hastily prepared in surrounding fields and common ground outside the city wall. Although few records remain to identify plague pit locations, over the centuries, through

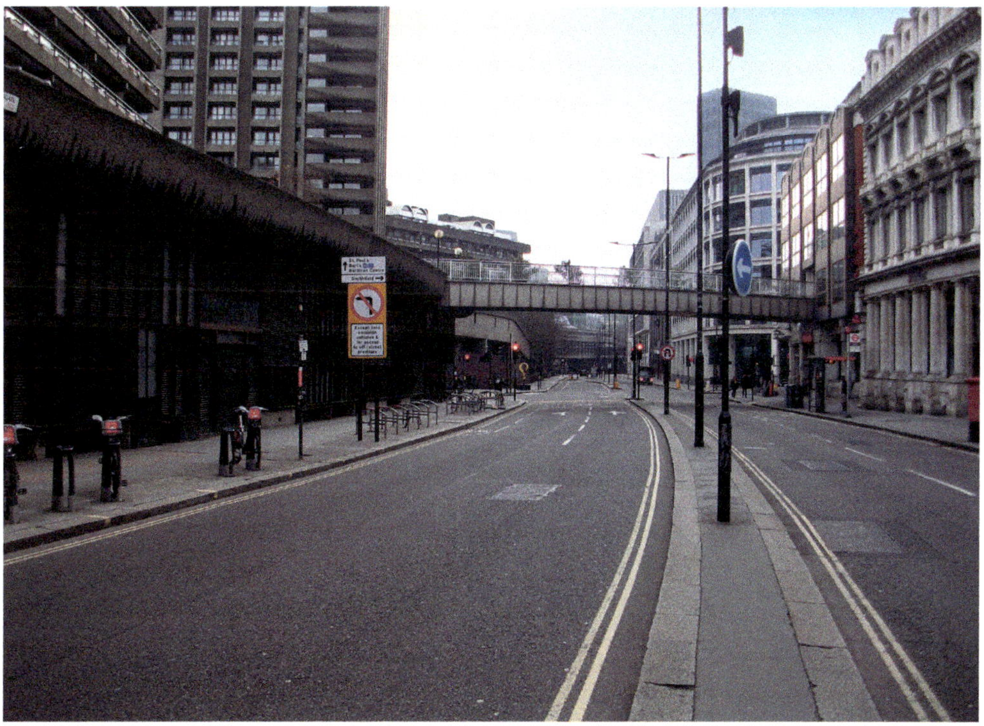

Aldersgate Street, EC1.

archaeological investigation, pits have been discovered close to many of London's most deprived districts, including Spitalfields and Whitechapel.

One burial pit, from an early outbreak of the plague, was discovered near Brushfield Street during the 1980s, where before the pandemic lockdown people were socialising in Spitalfields Market's lively bars, cafés, and restaurants, a short distance away from London's plague victims.

On the boundary line of Middlesex, Brushfield Street runs south of the market, west to east, towards the Nicholas Hawksmoor-designed Christ Church. Established as a vegetable market in the late 1600s under a licence granted by Charles II, Spitalfields, which takes its name from a twelfth-century hospital and priory, St Mary's Spittel, became notable for meat, poultry, and roots. The streets around the market developed into the centre of the silk-weaving industry when Huguenot refugees settled outside the city boundary to avoid its strict legislative regulations.

After the decline of the silk industry, when silk could be imported much cheaper than making it in London, they were supplanted by a community of Jewish textile workers. By the late nineteenth century, the houses once occupied by wealthy merchants had fallen into a state of disrepair and Spitalfields had become an urban slum, known as a den for London's criminal class, pickpockets, robbers, and pimps.

Acquired by the City of London Corporation, Spitalfields was converted into a wholesale fruit market, and after relocation to Leyton the old site went through a period of refurbishment and modernisation, receiving an award for the 'Best Private Market' in 2011.

Laid out along the line of Essex Street, the southern end of Commercial Street was built as part of the slum clearances during the mid-1800s to connect Spitalfields Market to

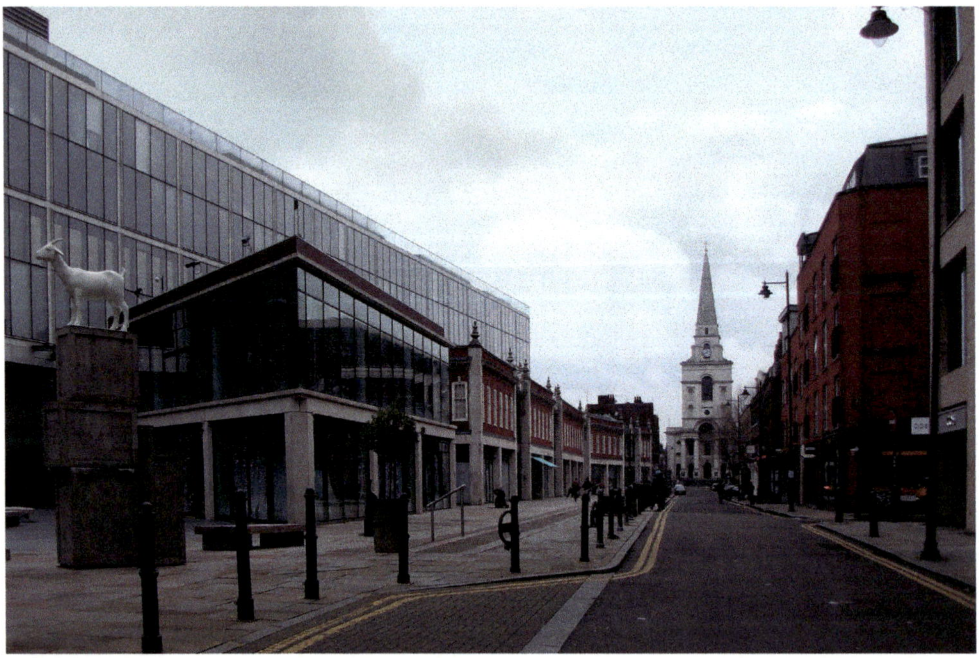

Brushfield Street, E1.

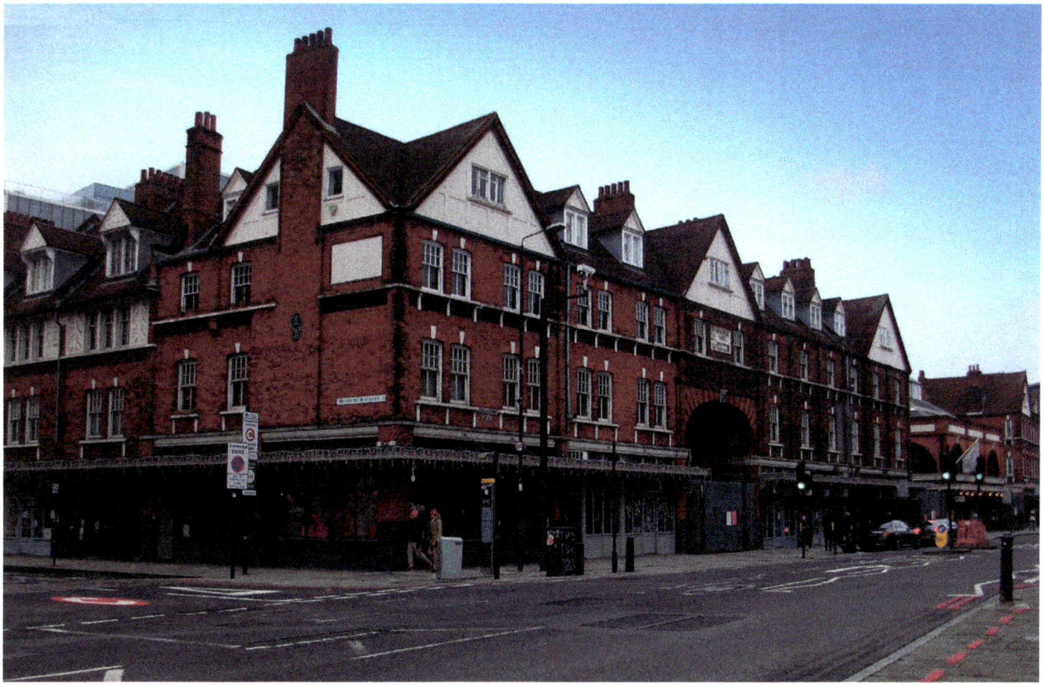

Commercial Street, EC1.

Whitechapel. The area was notorious for prostitutes; the Ten Bells public house, located on the corner of Fournier Street, was a popular place for ladies of the night to seek out clients.

Two of Jack the Ripper's victims, Mary Kelly and Annie Chapman, were reputed to have frequented the Ten Bells. The red-brick Horner Buildings, on the south-east corner of Spitalfields Market, were erected during the late 1800s, commissioned by the last private owner of the market, Robert Horner. Before lockdown, the old market hosted a huge variety of vintage, arts, and craft stalls.

Since the late 1800s, Whitechapel has been associated with a series of killings carried out by Jack the Ripper, a period when the East End was one of the worst slums in London and a place where many people from the City of London feared to go. All but one of the six women killed were prostitutes – there would have been over a thousand ladies of the night working on the streets at the time of the assaults. The murders took place over a period of three months in an area roughly covering a square mile north and south of Whitechapel High Street and Whitechapel Road. Several other murders were also attributed to Jack the Ripper, but as the assailant was never caught the total number of victims has never been established.

Until its closure in 2017, Whitechapel Bell Foundry, occupying eighteenth-century buildings on the corner of Whitechapel Road and Fieldgate Street, cast many of London's church bells, which were rung as a death knell or funeral toll for victims of the plague. Making bells in Whitechapel since the late 1500s, the foundry relocated during the mid-1700s to the site previously occupied by the Old Artichoke Ale House. Whitechapel cast bells for St Paul's, Canterbury Cathedral, Westminster Abbey, and the National Cathedral Washington.

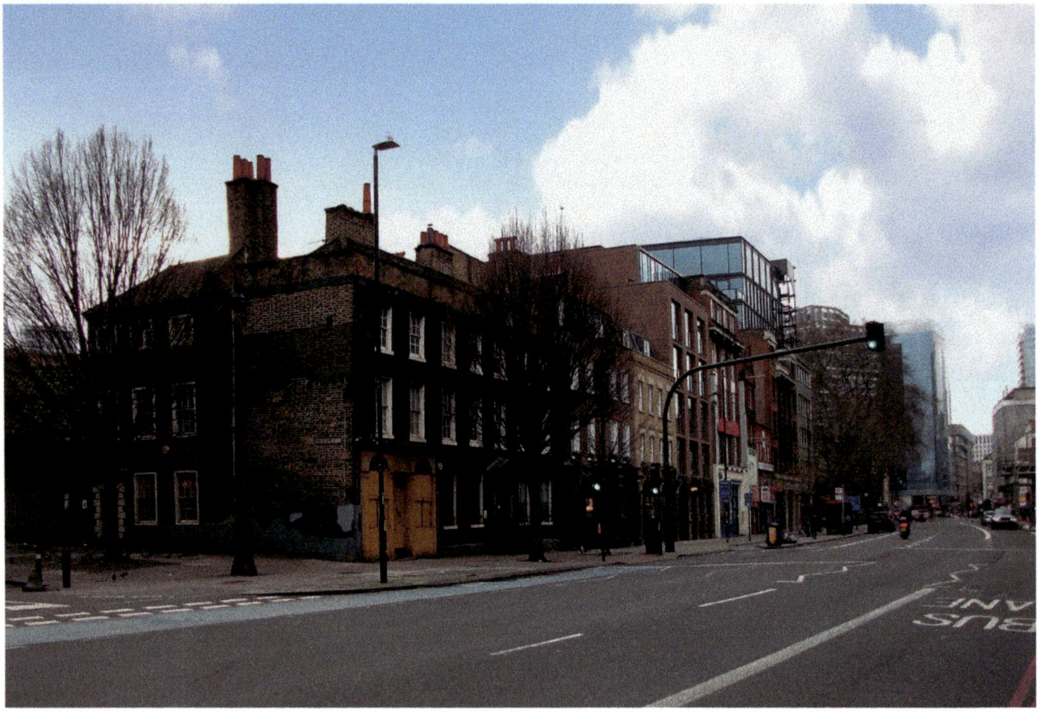

Whitechapel Road, E1.

Big Ben, which currently chimes from the Elizabeth Tower, Westminster, and America's Liberty Bell were also cast at the foundry. After the outbreak of the Second World War, the foundry made ammunition for Britain's forces, and when hostilities ceased was kept busy casting new church bells to replace those destroyed or damaged during bombing raids over London.

Throughout the eighteenth century, London's largest used-clothes market was held in Rosemary Lane, now Mint Street, in the district of Whitechapel – famous for the clothing industry known as the 'Rag Trade'.

Just a short walk away from where the poor resided in slum conditions was the Royal Mint, previously housed at the Tower of London, where all of the country's coinage was made prior to relocating to Wales in 1967. Much of the northside of Rosemary Lane was swept away during the slum clearances and when the London and Blackwall railway line was built.

Whitechapel was one of the districts worst affected by the plague during the seventeenth century, with many of the victims buried in pits at nearby Aldgate, and then by cholera outbreaks in the 1800s. When London was struck by outbreaks of the Black Death, two burial grounds were opened at East Smithfield between 1347 and 1351 to take the city's dead, where an estimated 200 victims were laid to rest each day during the plague outbreaks.

Once known as Smoothfield, during the thirteenth century a Pentecost fair was held on the level strip of land situated to the east of the city wall. Historically part of the parish

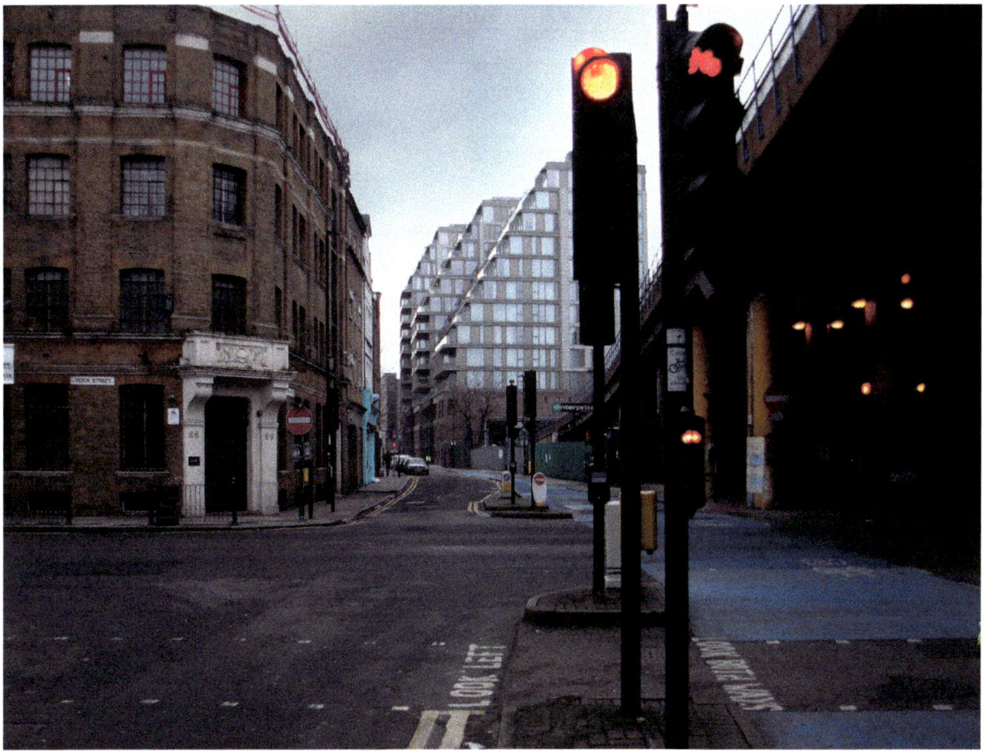

Royal Mint Street, E1.

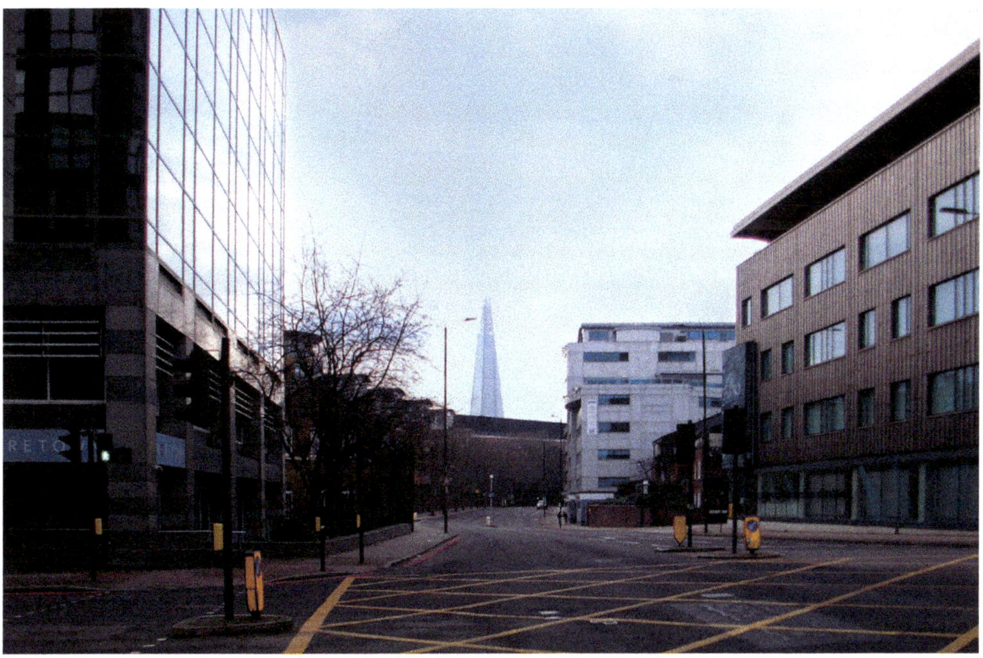

East Smithfield, E1.

of St Botolph-without-Aldgate, administration came under control of the liberties of the Tower of London in the late seventeenth century.

To south of the thoroughfare a succession of religious houses were established, including the Hospital of St Katharine, founded by Queen Matilda, cousin of King Stephen of England.

To the east of the Tower of London, the lawless liberty of St Katharine consisted of over a thousand small houses, several taverns, a brewery, and a hospital and church dedicated to St Katharine, an area home to an assemblage of vagabonds, pilferers, and prostitutes. Although plague mortality was half that of neighbouring areas to the north and east, during the early 1800s under the squalid and unsanitary conditions people were living there were frequent outbreaks of diseases such as cholera.

Through an Act of Parliament, in the face of protests, all the properties were demolished to create St Katharine Dock, designed by Thomas Telford. Accessed from the Thames by a lock, the dock handled and stored imported goods including tea, sugar, rubber, and wool.

Successful for only a short period, as large ships were unable to enter the narrow lock entrance, the warehouses around the east basin were destroyed in an air raid during the Blitz. The dock eventually closed in the early 1960s as it was no longer fit for purpose.

Gradually, most of the old warehouses were taken down and replaced by modern office buildings, apartments, private residencies, a hotel, bars, and restaurants. The basins of the dock were transformed into a marina for private vessels.

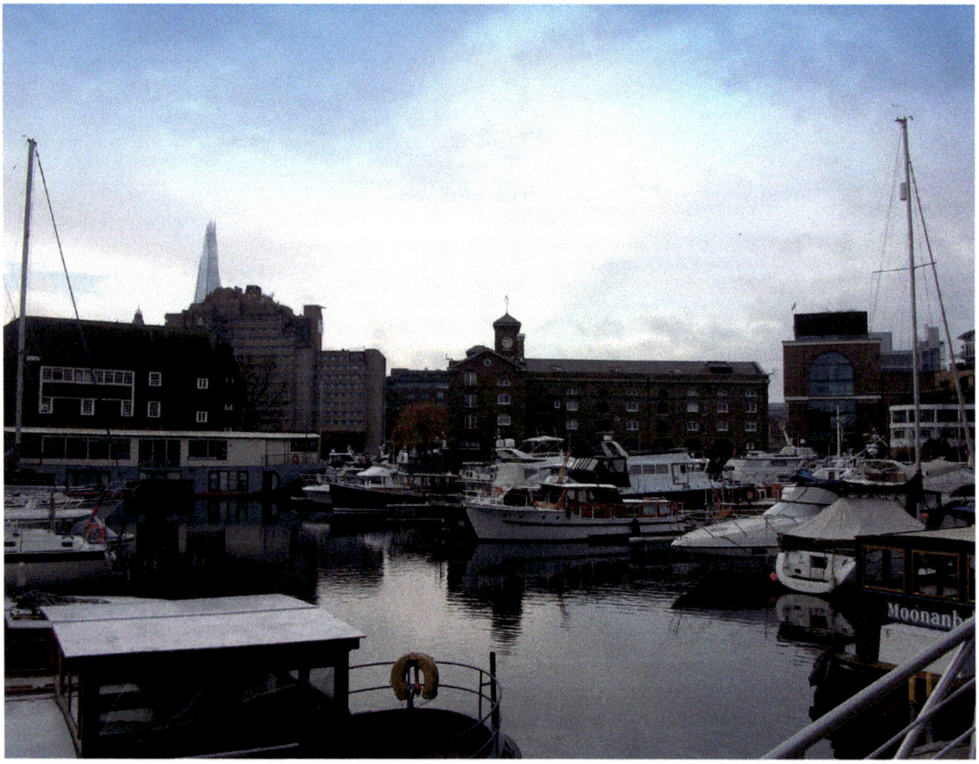

St Katharine Dock, E1.

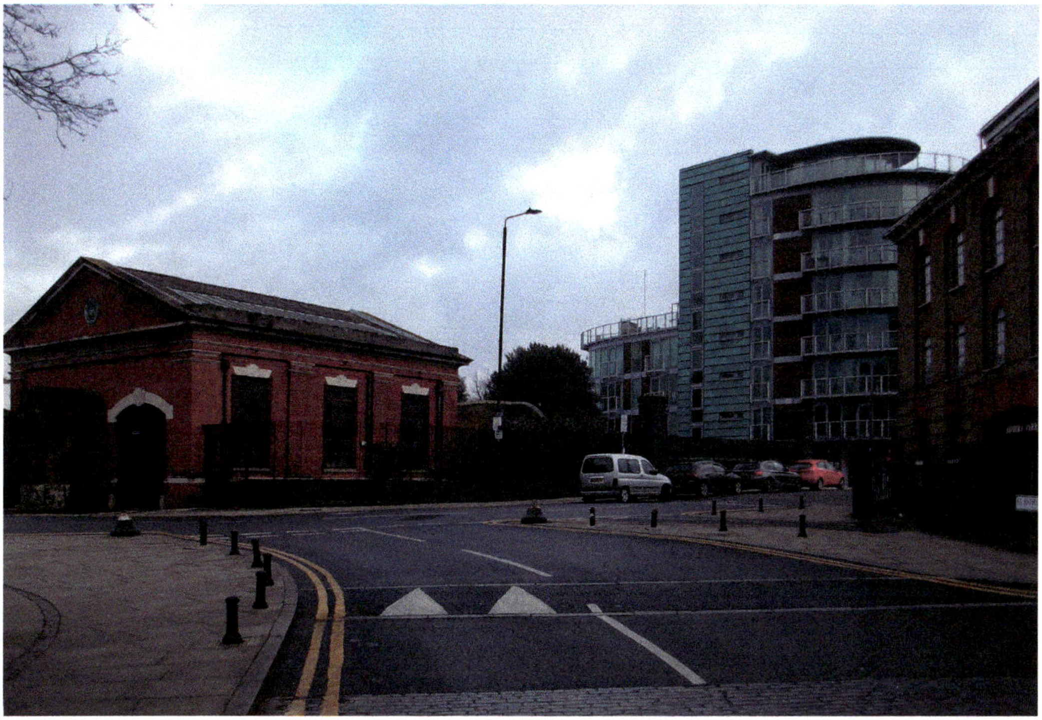

St Katharine's Way, E1.

The riverside streets around St Katharine Dock were extremely busy with people before lockdown, especially at weekends. Walkers and cyclists headed to and from the dock, along St Kartharine's Way, and past the old Port of London dock house, one of the few remaining dockside buildings to survive the redevelopment of the docks in the 1970s.

The main route towards Wapping, St Katharine's Way, was once a thriving waterfront workplace, with warehouses, workshops, and stores on each side. The riverfront warehouses which survived the Blitz were refurbished to provide exclusive apartments, while to the north, London Dock, and the dockland basins, were redeveloped into a large residential estate.

Wapping High Street, running parallel to the River Thames, was once an area of open marshland built upon during the late sixteenth century after the marsh was drained and a wall erected along the river embankment. The highway, and its side streets and alleys, were made up of quickly erected tenements and small cottages inhabited by sailors and tradesmen, alongside stores and workshops associated with shipping and seafaring. By the mid-1700s, there were thirty-six taverns on Wapping High Street, one of the most famous, the Prospect of Whitby, named after a collier, claims to be the oldest tavern on the river, dating to the early 1500s.

Another tavern, the Town of Ramsgate, also has a long heritage. Its present mid-eighteenth-century, Grade II listed building was erected on the site of a much older sixteenth-century inn. Situated between Wapping New Stairs and King Edward's Stairs is Execution Dock where pirates were once hung, close to the headquarters of Thames River Police, England's first police force formed in 1798.

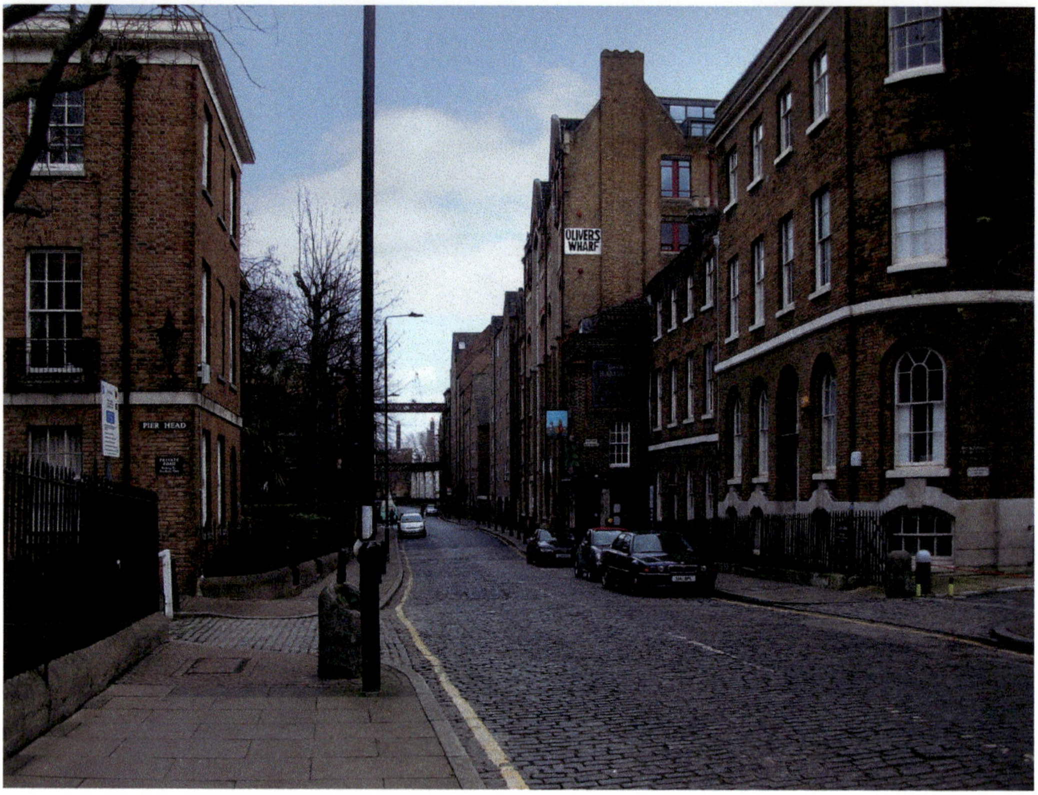

Wapping High Street, E1.

As the Great Plague spread through the city, many fled to the suburbs of Poplar, Limehouse and Wapping, believing they would be safe from infection; however, in doing so the plague travelled with them and the first deaths occurred in early July 1666. The area of Wapping (one of London's poorest districts) was heavily bombed during the Second World War, and after the closure of the docks Wapping High Street became particularly neglected, remaining in a rundown state until the 1980s, when the warehouses and riverside houses were refurbished and transformed into highly sought-after domestic residences.

At the outbreak of the Great Fire only one bridge crossed the Thames, and although some the properties on London Bridge burned down, the fire never reached the emerging communities on the South Bank. Once part of Kent and Surrey, and outside the administration of the City of London, from the Middle Ages onwards the districts along the South Bank evolved as notorious self-administered places of entertainment, where cockfighting and bear-baiting became a popular attraction and lively plays were performed to rowdy theatre audiences at the Swan, the Rose, and the Globe.

Although safe from the fire, the parishes on the South Bank did not escape the plague. Victims were buried alongside paupers, criminals, and thousands of prostitutes at Cross Bones, an unconsecrated graveyard. Over the following three centuries, the South Bank developed into an area dominated by industry and trade where warehouses, docks, and workshops were built along the river frontage, and several new bridges were constructed

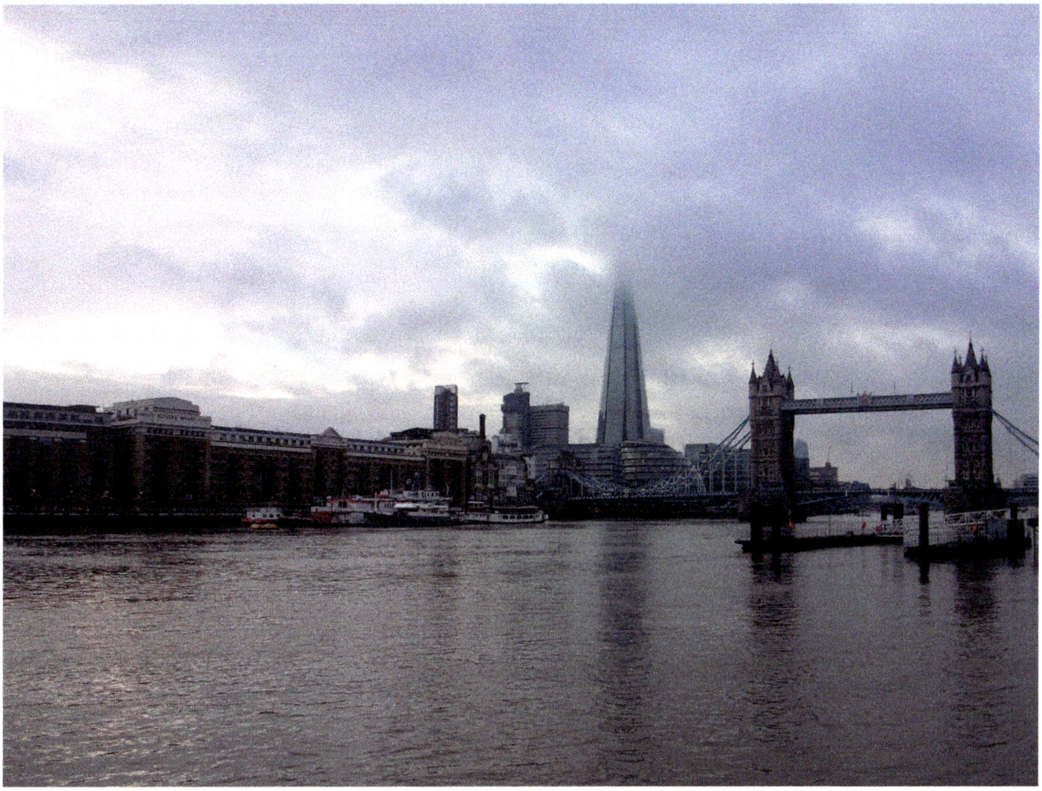

Tower Bridge, E1.

to move goods and people across the river; the Gothic-style Tower Bridge was built between 1886 and 1894.

Riverside industries from Bermondsey to Southwark came under intensive bombing during the Blitz, the fires from goods stored in warehouses – pepper, rum, lumber, and rubber – sending plumes of fume-filled toxic smoke billowing out across London. Much of the South Bank came under redevelopment during the mid-1900s. The seventy-two-storey Shard, the tallest building in the United Kingdom, completed in 2012, is one of many ultra-modern developments on the South Bank, which once again became a place noted for its entertainment and arts, visited annually by millions of people up until the pandemic lockdown.

Back across the river, to the west of the city, the more prosperous areas of London were also affected by early outbreaks of the plague. Both the wealthy and the poor lived in close proximity, the mansions and town houses surrounded by tenements and slums. Close to St Giles, where the Great Plague epidemic began, the adjacent parish of St Martin-in-the-Fields recorded over 200 deaths from the plague in the summer of 1665, the parish occupying a large area from Leicester Square west to Constitution Hill and south as far as Charing Cross.

The present rail bridge spanning the river between Charing Cross station and Waterloo station to the south replaced Isambard Kingdom Brunel's Hungerford Rail Bridge, named

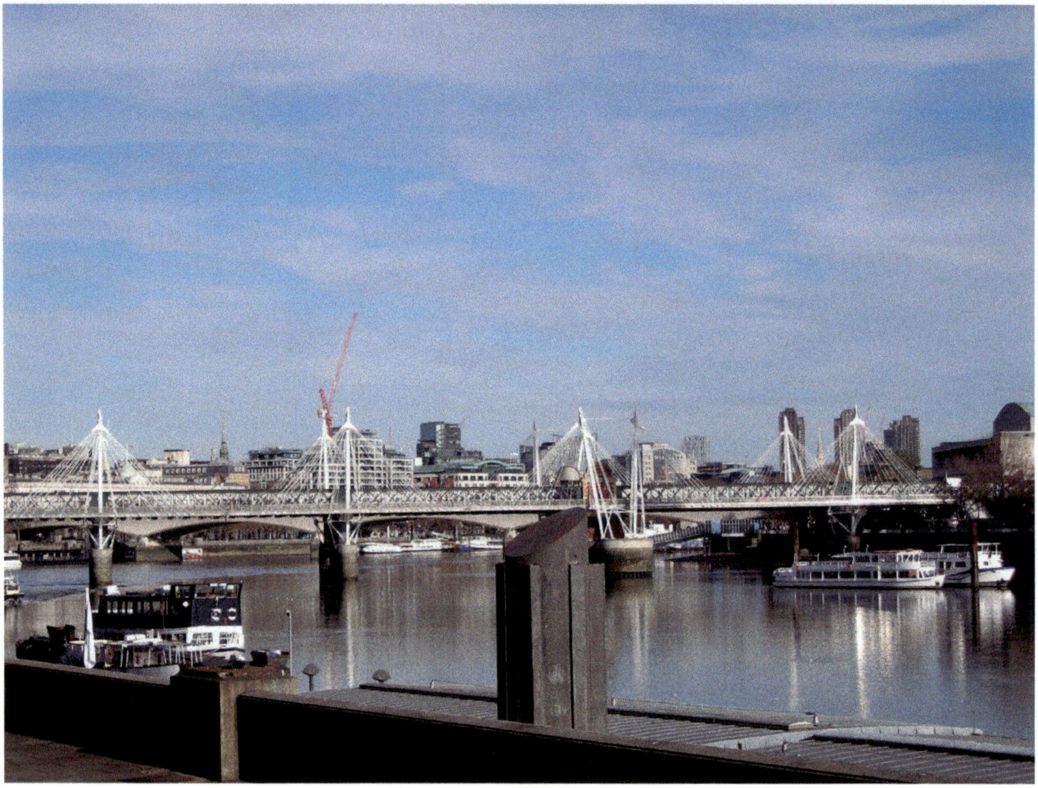

Hungerford and Golden Jubilee bridges, WC2.

after Hungerford Market. The second rail bridge had pedestrian walks added each side, and after the upstream walkway was removed when the railway was widened, a temporary walkway was erected in 1951 for use during the Festival of Britain.

Repaired and refurbished many times, the walkways were replaced and named the Golden Jubilee Bridges in 2002, to honour Queen Elizabeth II's then fifty-year reign. It is estimated 8.5 million people use the walkways annually; however, during lockdown the footfall fell considerably.

Further to the west of the parish of St Giles, Great Russell Street was built on the grounds of a former leper hospital. One of its buildings once occupied a site on the corner of Museum Street, opposite the British Museum's main entrance. Much of the land was owned by the Russell family, who leased out a section in 1662 to build a row of smart properties, which became Great Russell Street. On the death of Sir Hans Sloane, an Anglo-Irish physician, naturalist and collector, his assembly of books, manuscripts, and curiosities were bequeathed to George II, who gave royal assent for Parliament to establish a British Museum.

The trustees acquired Montagu House on Great Russell Street, converting the mansion into a museum for the display and storage of thousands of artefacts. In the early 1800s, Montagu House was no longer large enough to exhibit the collections, and after it was demolished a grand new neoclassical building was erected in its place. Although the

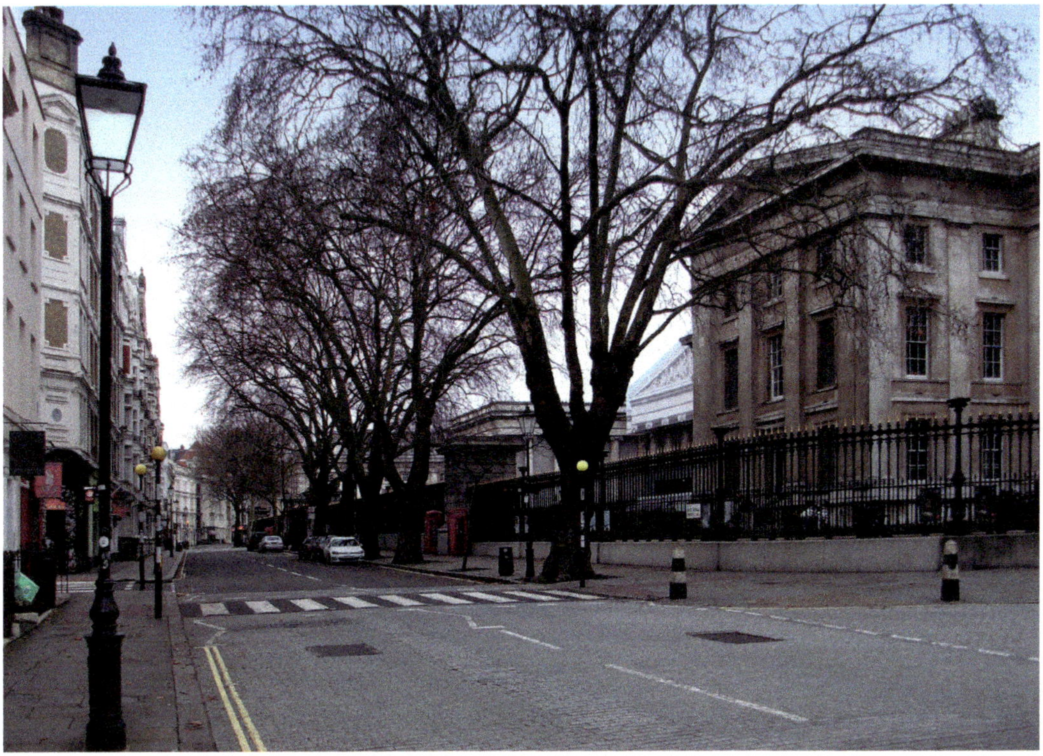

Great Russell Street, WC1.

building was damaged during the Blitz all the museum's contents had been removed for safe storage, only being returned once the repairs were complete.

One of many districts towards the north-west of London was the Bloomsbury estate, a development of properties built for wealthy middle-class residents. Five lodges and gates were built around the boundary in the early 1800s to keep pedestrians and traffic out. At Upper Woburn Place, named after Woburn Abbey, the seat of the Duke of Bedford (who created much of Bloomsbury), the gate was still in use up until the nineteenth century.

An area of wasteland behind houses on Upper Woburn Place was converted into lawn tennis courts for the use of the estate's wealthy tenants. Upper Woburn Place evolved into a busy main thoroughfare, leading from Euston Road towards Holborn, where several large, impressive buildings were erected in the early 1900s.

The red-brick building on the east side of the road, now home to the British Medical Association, was first designed for the Theosophical Society. When construction was interrupted by the outbreak of the First World War, and the society was unable to continue to fund the project, the building was acquired by the BMA.

The south end of Upper Woburn Place suffered bomb damage during the Second World War when several high-explosive bombs fell across Bloomsbury in 1941, one falling directly on the southern end of Upper Woburn Place. In July 2006, when acts of terrorism broke out across London, a bomb planted on a double-decker bus travelling south on Upper Woburn Place exploded. The blast killed thirteen passengers and wounded many others.

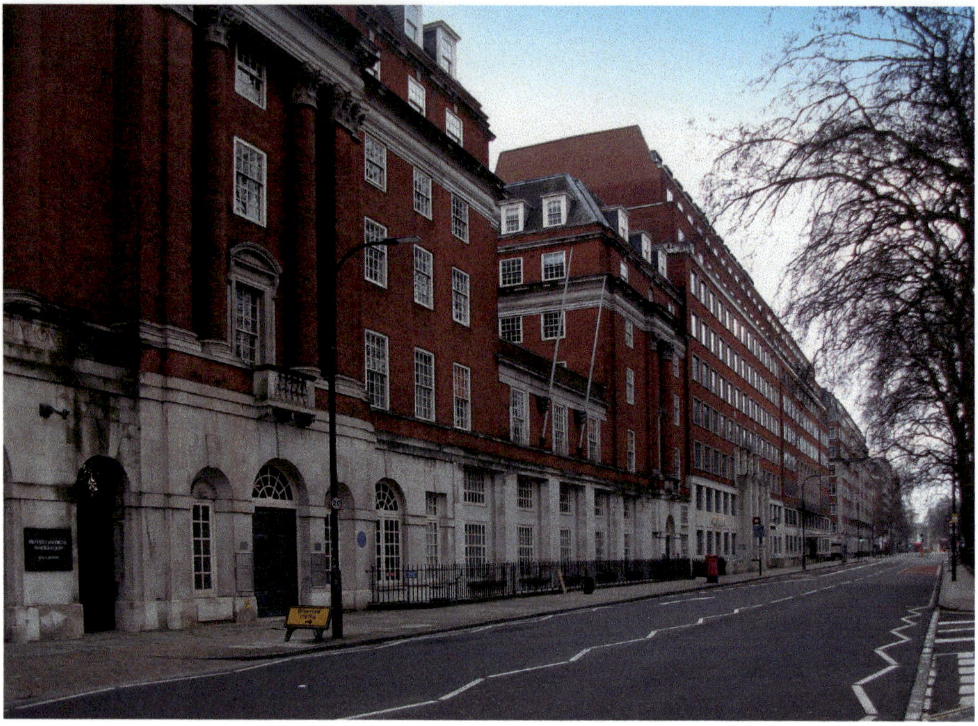

Upper Woburn Place, WC1.

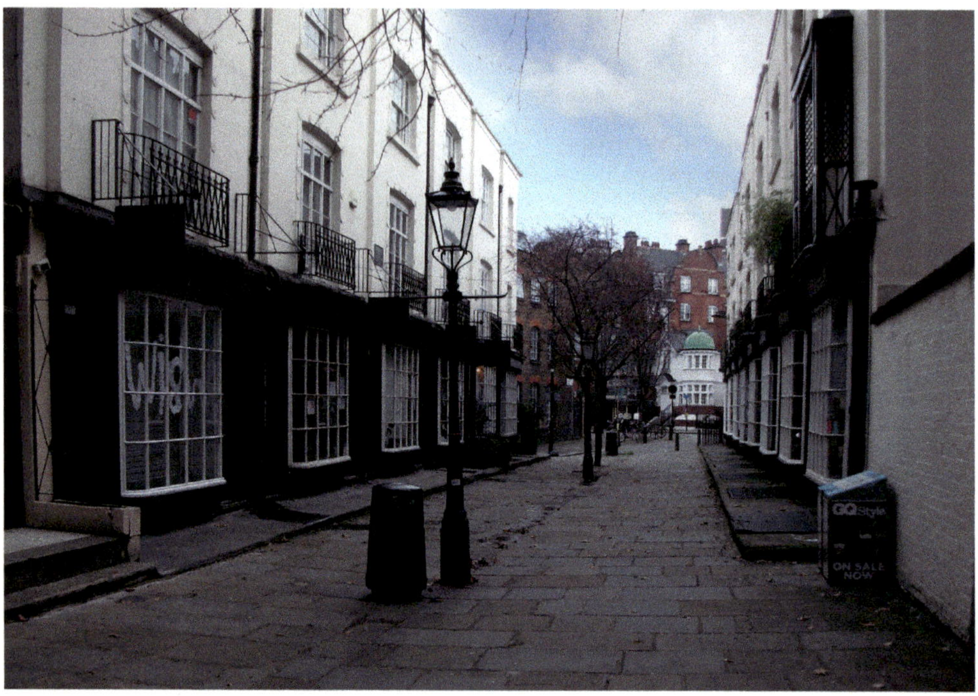

Woburn Walk, WC2.

To the north of Upper Woburn Place, a secluded pedestrian street formerly known as Woburn Buildings is one of London's finest early examples of a Georgian shopping area. It was designed by architect Thomas Cubitt, responsible for buildings in Belgravia and Pimlico. The stucco-fronted, three-storey shops with accommodation above share the same design as several properties on Duke's Road, running northwards to Euston Road.

Notable residents of Woburn Walk include Irish poet and dramatist William Butler Yeats, novelist Dorothy Richardson, and radical journalist and reformer George Holyoake, who lived above a newsagent. Located away from London's well-trodden tourist routes, with little passing trade, the row of well-preserved independently run shops have somehow managed to survive, but following the introduction of lockdown all were forced to temporarily close.

Ralph Montagu, the 1st Duke of Montagu and Charles II's ambassador to Paris, had a large mansion built on part of the Bedford estate, then owned by the Russell family. After Herbrand Russell, 11th Duke of Bedford, succeeded to the title in 1893 he began selling off parts of the estate. The University of London and the British Museum now occupy two areas to the west of Montague Street, named after the demolished Montagu House.

The street's houses, almost all Grade II listed, were built on the gardens of Montagu House between 1803 and 1806, designed by James Burton, the most successful property developer of Regency and Georgian London. The residents were some of the wealthiest and most privileged members of London society. By the early 1900s many of these houses were converted into lodgings and small hotels.

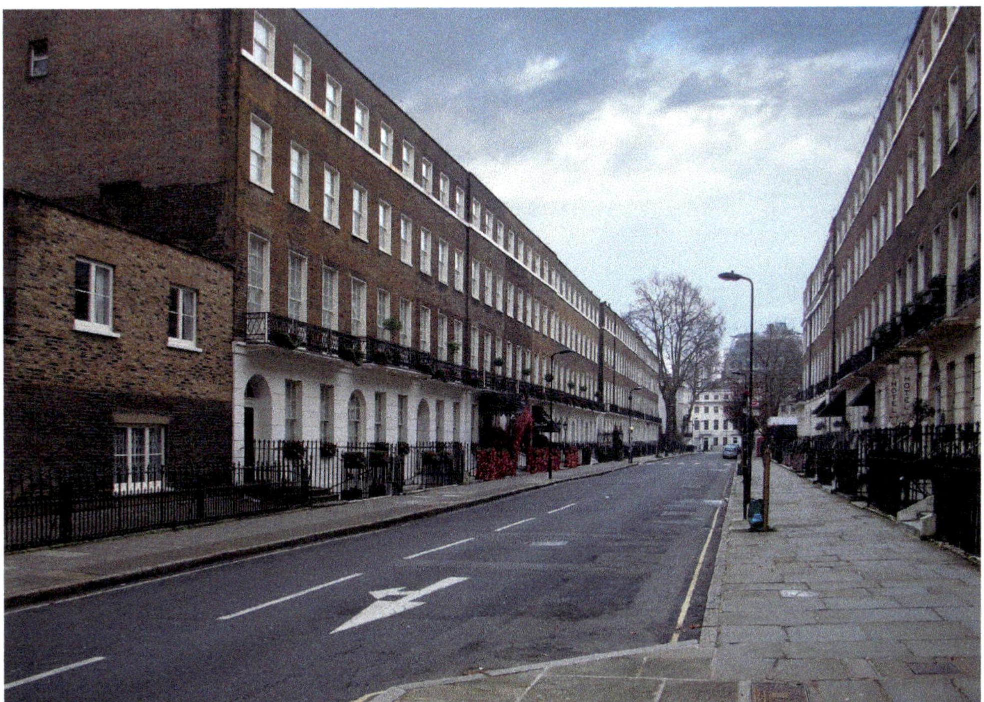

Montague Street, WC1.

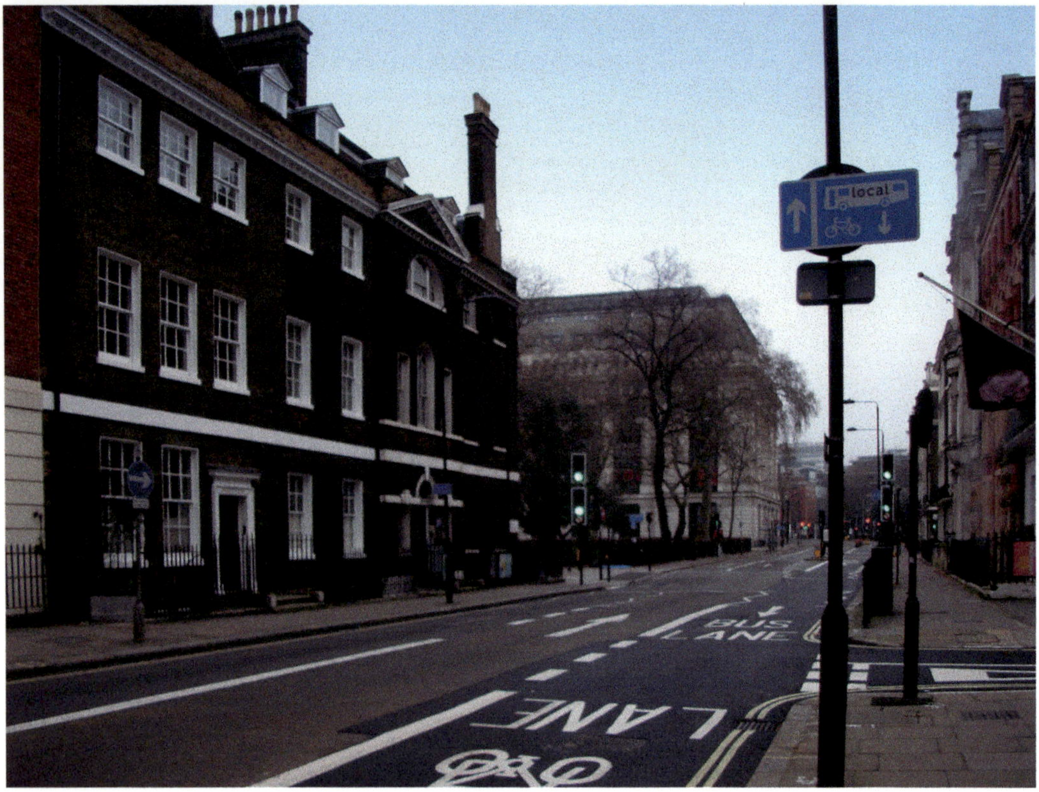

Bloomsbury Way, WC1.

Running from New Oxford Street to Bloomsbury Square, Bloomsbury Way makes up part of the south boundary of land developed in the seventeenth century by the earls of Southampton, and later the Duke of Bedford. Once the manor grounds held by the Blemund family during the thirteenth century, Bloomsbury evolved into a prosperous Regency residential district, the location of a number of cultural and educational institutions.

Bloomsbury Square, known originally as Southampton Square, was one of the earliest of London's many formal squares. Lined with high, elegant, terraced properties, residents included writer Issac D'Israeli, playwright Richard Steel, and barrister and politician William Murray, 1st Earl of Mansfield.

London's largest square and one of the capital's busiest landmarks was laid out in the mid-1800s on the King's Mews, where Edward I kept hunting hawks. Trafalgar Square was created to commemorate the Battle of Trafalgar, and for centuries before was where all distances from London were measured – at a point where the statue of Charles I now stands, the original site of Charing Cross. As the land formed a natural slope, the project's architect, Sir Charles Barry, levelled and paved the lower ground and erected a higher terrace to the north, accessed by steps on each side.

During excavations the remains of lions, rhinoceroses, and elephants were discovered, dating to the interglacial period. Trafalgar Square became a popular meeting place for

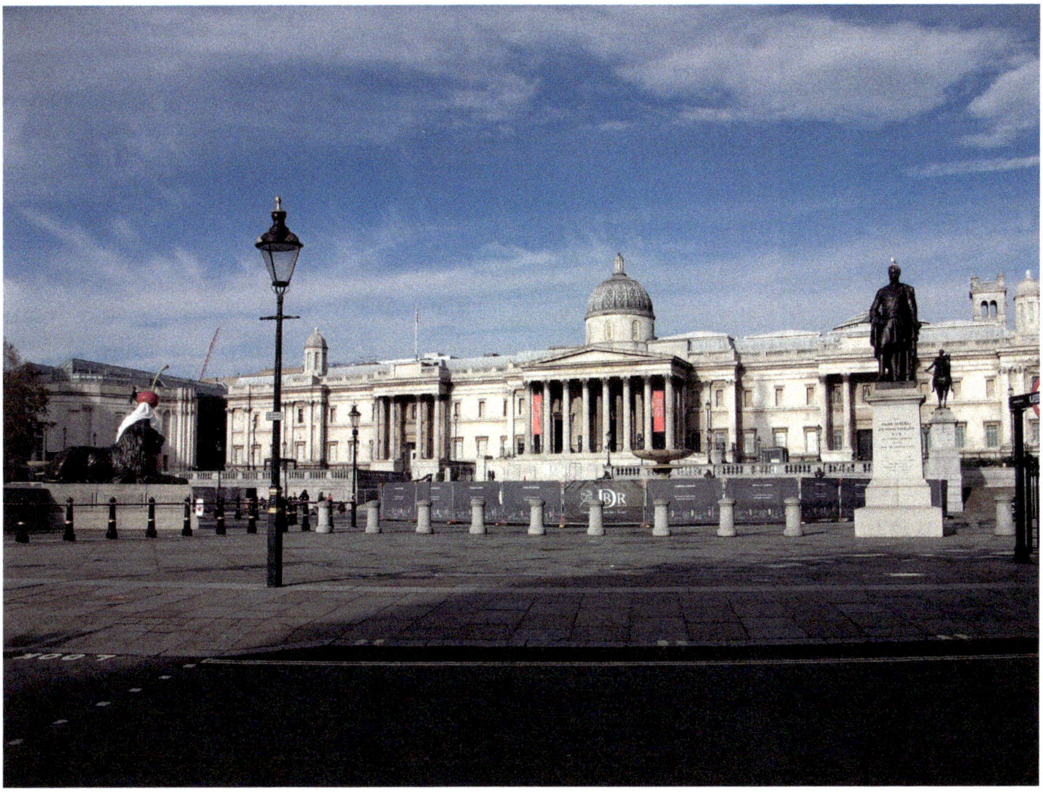

Trafalgar Square, WC2.

political gatherings and demonstrations. In 1887, around 10,000 protestors confronted 2,000 police officers and 400 troops to protest over unemployment and coercion in Ireland.

Tourists came to feed hundreds of pigeons flocking around the square's statues and fountains up until the early 2000s, when licensed bird feed sellers were closed down and it became a criminal offence to feed the birds. Although there are now fewer pigeons to be seen at Trafalgar Square, there were even fewer people visiting this popular landmark during lockdown.

At the centre of Trafalgar Square, Nelson's Column rises 145 feet into the air, topped by a stone statue of Admiral Lord Nelson. Designed by William Railton, the monument was constructed forty-five years after Nelson's final naval engagement, where he was shot and mortally wounded aboard HMS *Victory*.

The sculpture of Nelson was carved by Edward Hodges Baily and the four huge, identical, bronze Barbary lions situated at the column's base were designed by Sir Edward Landseer. On each side of the pedestal the bronze bas-reliefs, depicting scenes of the battle, were cast from guns captured during Nelson's battles.

It is believed that if Adolf Hitler's plan to invade Britain had been successful, Nelson's Column would have been relocated to Berlin. The column has been climbed on various occasions as publicity stunts. In 2016, an activist from Greenpeace managed to ascend the column and place a large protective face mask over Nelson's nose and mouth to raise awareness of the increasing levels of air pollution.

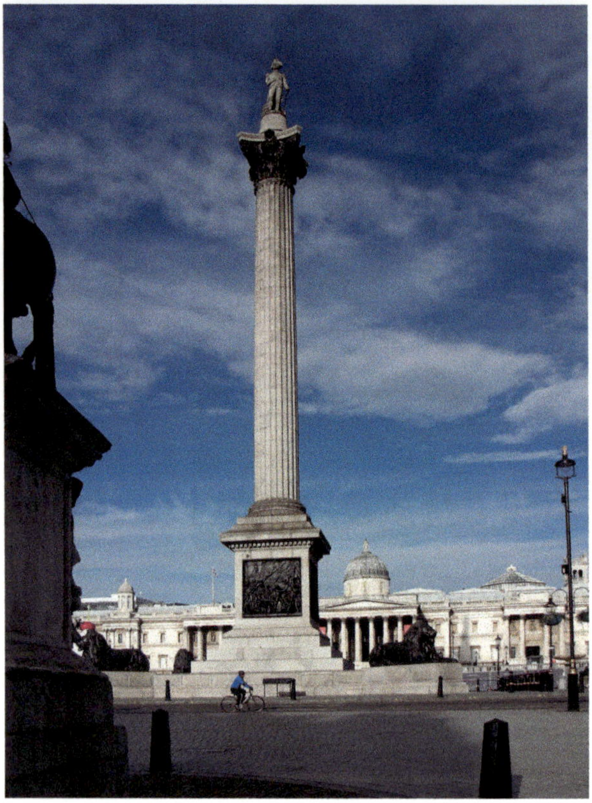

Nelson's Column, WC2.

To the north of Trafalgar Square the National Gallery, erected between 1832 and 1838, exhibits the nation's most notable paintings, the grand building replacing a much smaller gallery on Pall Mall. Many of the gallery's first paintings were purchased by the government at the behest of George VI. The gallery's principal director, Sir Charles Eastlake, acquired 139 works of art during several trips to Italy.

All the museum's paintings were removed for safe storage at the outbreak of the Second World War, and the empty galleries were used to perform musical recitals for the public to raise morale. Over many years various alterations and additions have been made to the gallery buildings, which now hold a collection of over 2,300 paintings.

Throughout the year, up until lockdown restrictions, an assembly of street artists performed on the terrace between the gallery and the square, entertaining the thousands of people who passed by daily, hoping for a donation of some loose change.

Tucked away behind Admiralty Arch, a little thoroughfare takes its name from an Elizabethan 'Spring Garden' once located in the grounds of Whitehall Palace. In the mid-seventeenth century, Spring Garden became a refuge for debtors including Sir Edward Hungerford, Member of Parliament and one of Oliver Cromwell's commanders during the Civil War – one of the most notorious who was forced to sell off his properties, including Hungerford Market.

Spring Garden's fortunes had turned around by the late 1600s, and for almost a century it became a fashionable place to live. The properties were laid out in two rows and

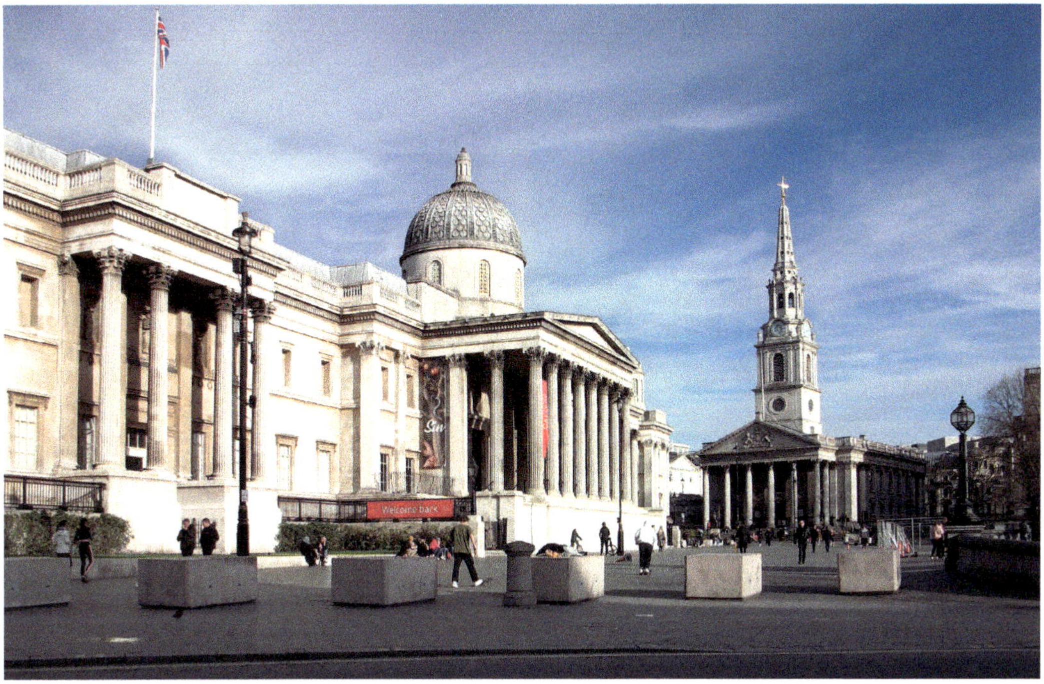

The National Gallery, WC2.

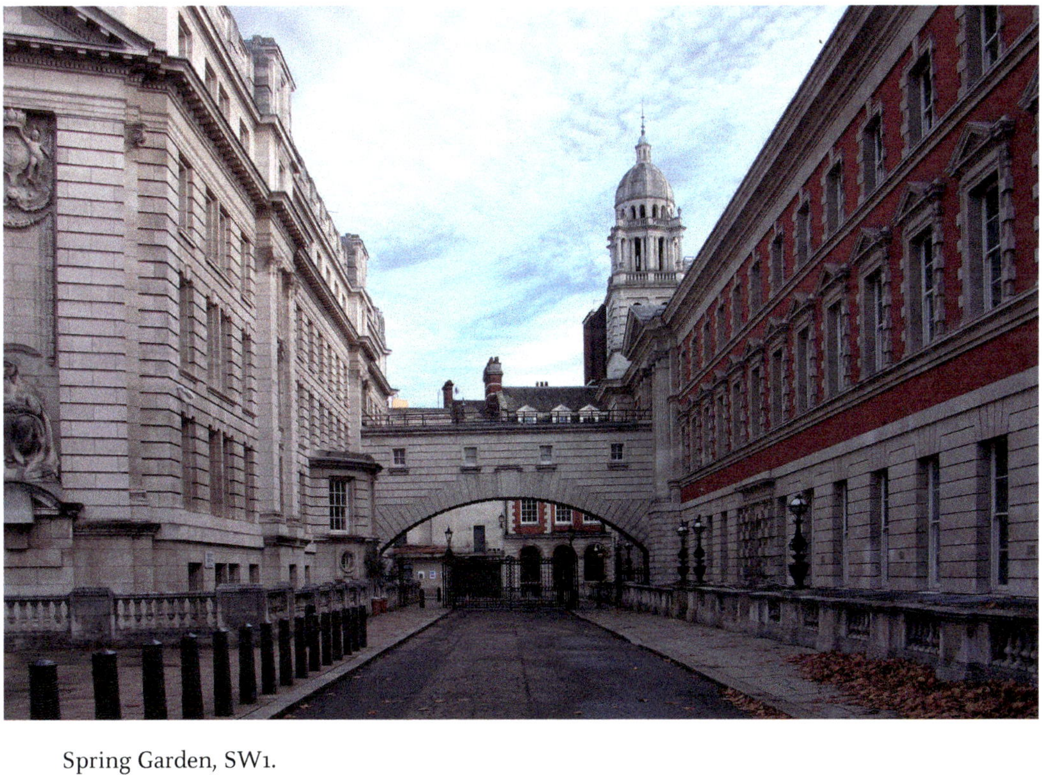

Spring Garden, SW1.

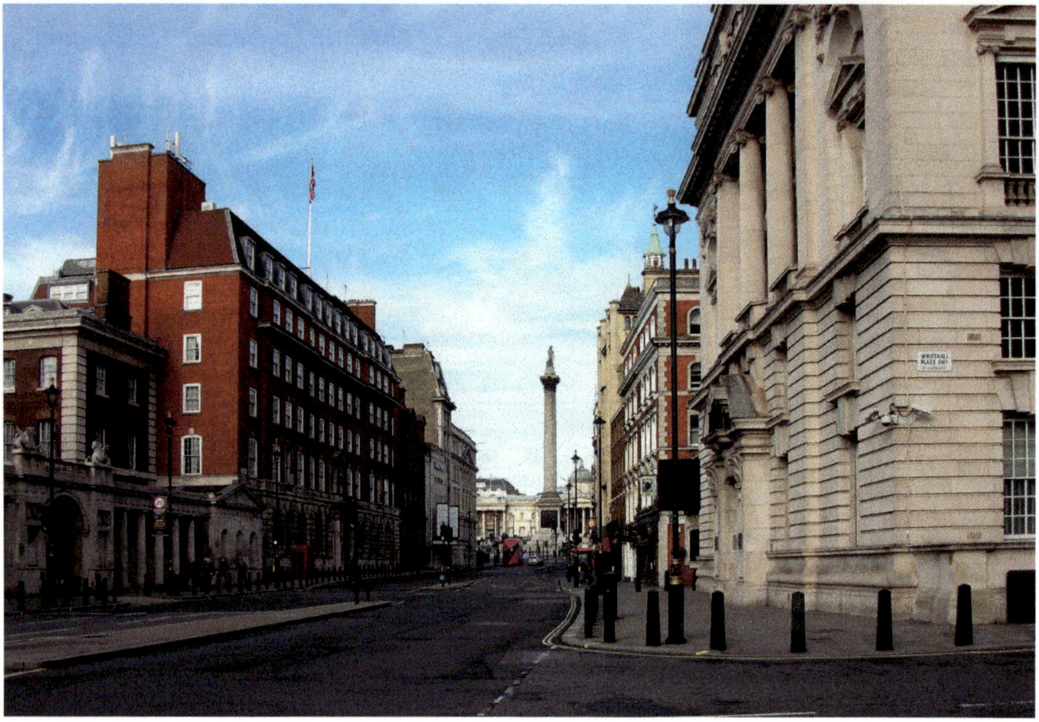

Whitehall, SW1.

included a chapel and a Great Room, which was used as a concert hall. The Admiralty Office acquired several of the buildings for use as offices, and by the late 1800s had taken over the whole site. Most of the area was cleared to erect Admiralty Arch and its adjoining buildings, which was opened in 1910.

The busy road known as Whitehall, running from Charing Cross to Westminster, has been in use since the Middle Ages. At one time Whitehall only applied to the northern end of the route leading from Whitehall Palace; then, when the palace burned down in 1698, the whole thoroughfare became known as Whitehall.

Made up mostly of residential properties between the sixteenth and seventeenth centuries, Whitehall, at the edge of urban London, became a popular place to live. When plague broke out in 1665, in an attempt to escape the epidemic, people hurried to Whitehall en mass to board coaches heading out of London.

During the worst period of the plague, Samuel Pepys sent his wife to Woolwich, but continued his work in his Whitehall Admiralty Office before joining her in the summer.

Through an increasing amount of traffic passing through Whitehall during the early eighteenth century, major alterations were carried out to widen the road by demolishing houses and blocks of residential properties lining the route. As private leases ran out on the existing buildings, ownership reverted to the crown and many were converted into public offices, and new government buildings were erected on the grounds of Whitehall Palace.

When the kings of Scotland and their representatives journeyed to London during the early 1500s to convene with English royalty, they were granted use of Whitehall Palace

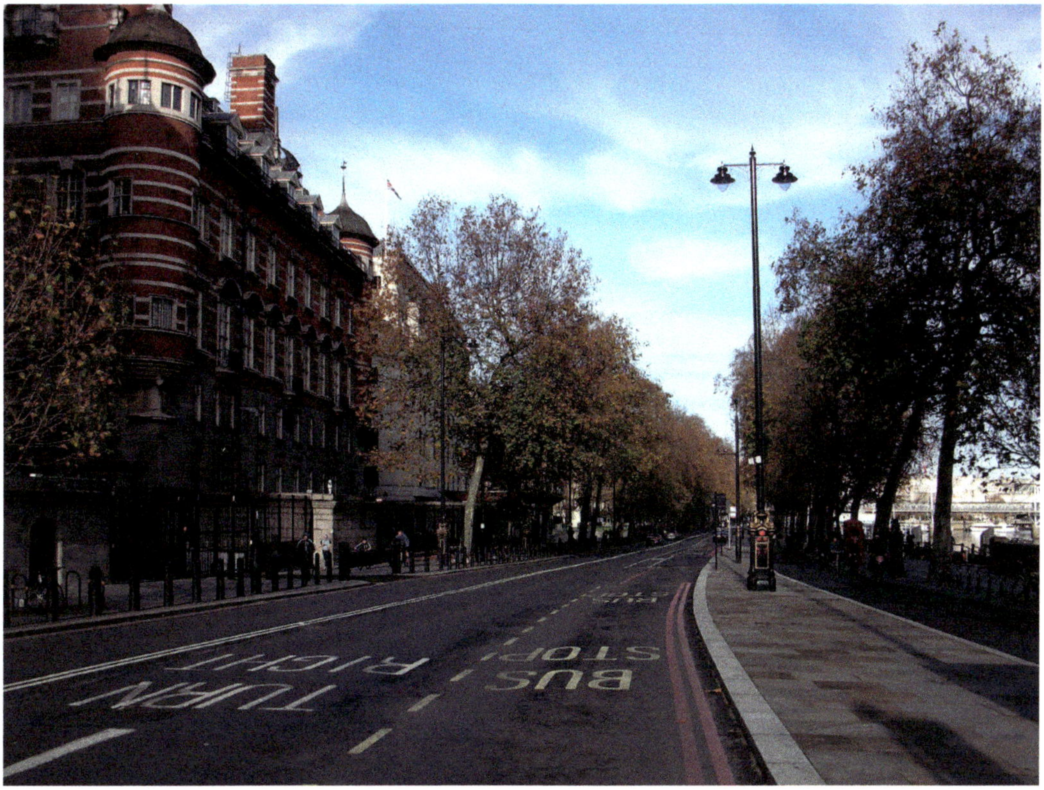

New Scotland Yard, SW1.

precincts. Other buildings later occupying the site included government and civil service offices and various official lodging houses.

On the formation of the Metropolitan police in 1829, a police commissioners' office was built at Whitehall Place, backing onto Great Scotland Yard, and over time adjoining buildings were occupied by the police. Eventually outgrowing their premises, when land was reclaimed after construction of the Victoria Embankment during the late 1800s, the Metropolitan Police headquarters, New Scotland Yard, was built on land originally reserved for the Grand National Opera House. During construction, the dismembered torso of a women was discovered in a recently built vault – one murder case the police weren't able to solve.

When all but the Banqueting Hall of Whitehall Palace was destroyed by fire, believed to have been started by a careless laundry woman, the site remained an expanse of wasteland up until the early eighteenth century when Robert Darcy, 3rd Earl of Holderness, leased part of the of site to build an impressive house.

Other properties were soon erected along the thoroughfare, which was named Whitehall Avenue. A large block of government offices were built to the north of Horse Guards Avenue, which has been occupied by the Ministry of Defence since 1964.

London has suffered a series of IRA bomb attacks. In 1991, the republicans fired a mortar at the prime minister's Downing Street residence from a van parked on the avenue. Although

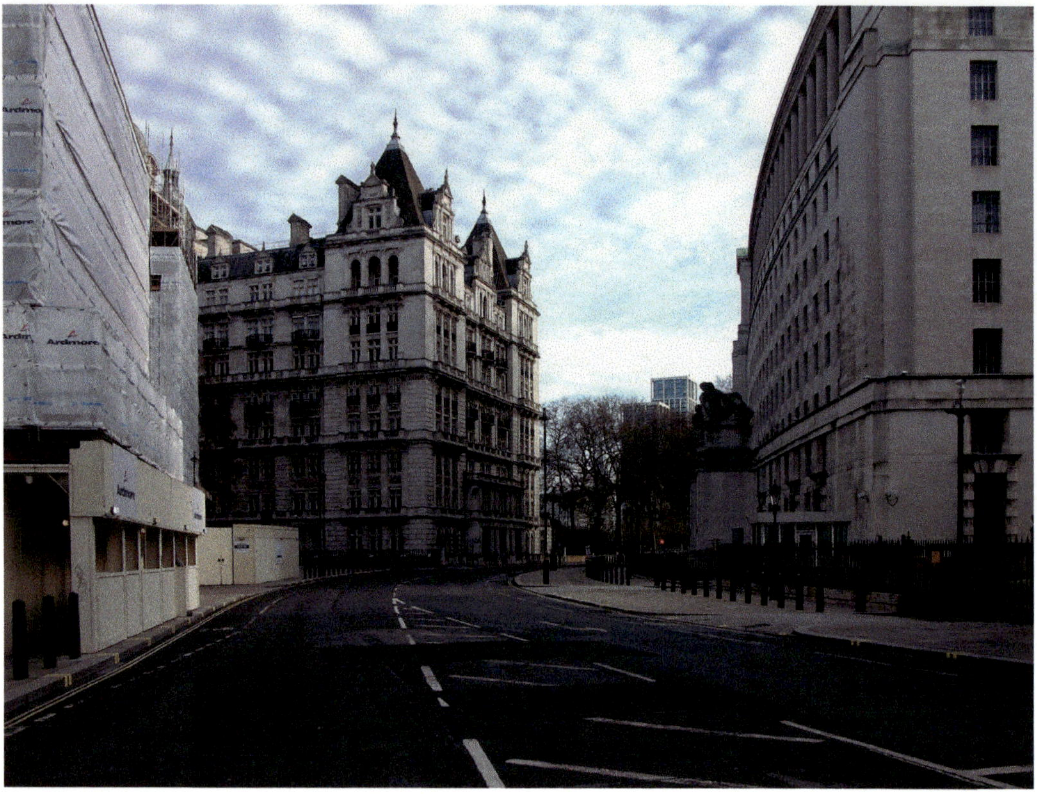

Horse Guards Avenue, SW1.

one bomb exploded in the garden of No. 10 Downing Street and two more landed on a green near the Foreign Office, no one was seriously injured. After the attack, vehicles were banned from parking on roads around Whitehall, which are all usually busy with traffic.

In 1649, a Tudor guardhouse was erected to the south of Whitehall Palace tilt yard, where Henry VIII held a great tournament in 1540. The guardhouse was replaced by a larger building in 1663 that was used as a barracks for the Horse Guards and Foot Guards, along with stables for horses.

The present guardhouse, designed by William Kent, was built between 1750 and 1758. It was situated at the original entrance to Whitehall Palace and guarded by two mounted troopers posted each day outside. The Household Cavalry Museum, which, like all of London's museums, closed to the public during lockdown, is located in a building behind the guardhouse where the horses are also stabled. At 4 p.m. every day an inspection of the guard takes place, a tradition introduced by Queen Victoria in 1894 after discovering the guards drinking and gambling while on afternoon duty.

Unveiled in 1920 to commemorate those who gave their lives in war and whose remains lay elsewhere, the stone-built Cenotaph, designed by architect Edward Lutyens, replaced a temporary memorial erected after the end of the First World War. The unveiling was part of a ceremonial procession for the unknown warrior laid to rest at Westminster Abbey. Whitehall was closed to traffic for several days to allow members of the public to file past

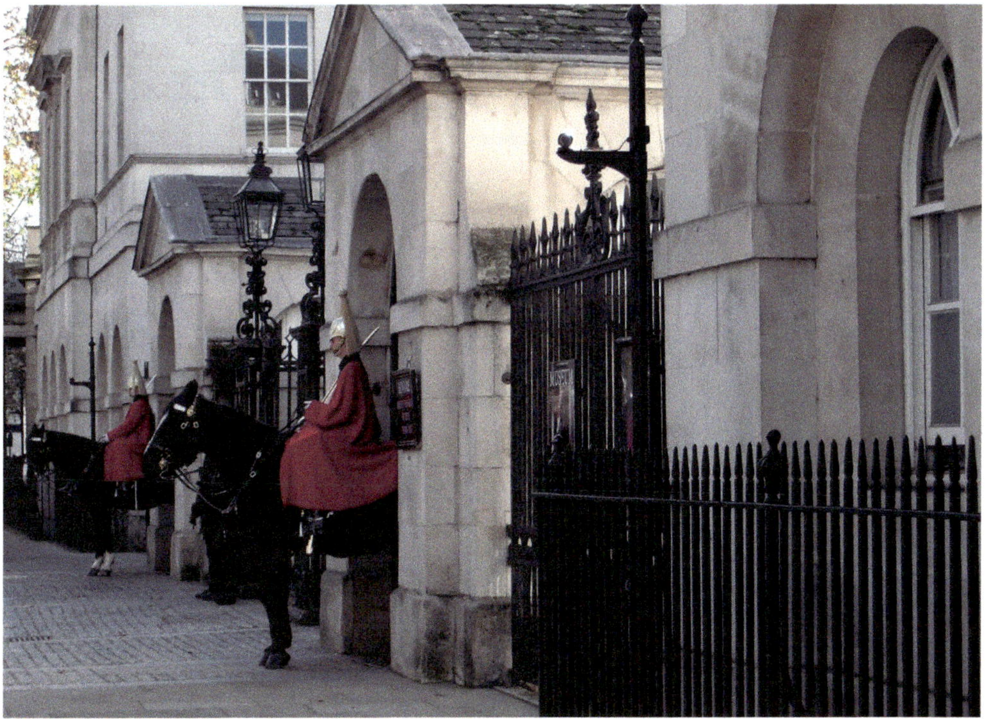

Horse Guards Parade, SW1.

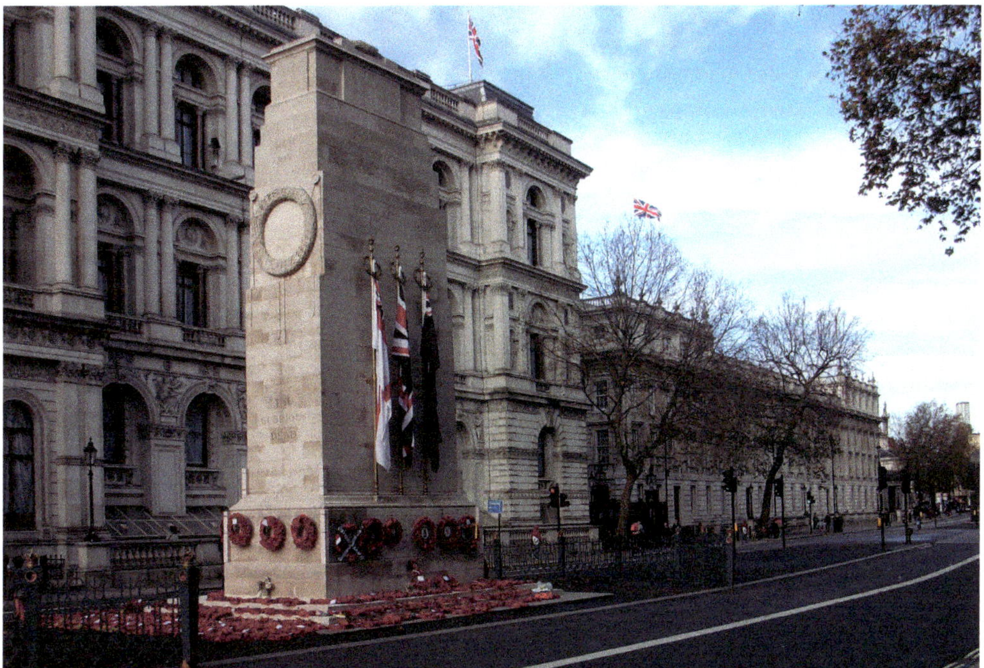

The Cenotaph, SW1.

and lay wreaths and flowers at the base of the Cenotaph. Although designated a Grade I listed building, the Cenotaph has been vandalised by political protestors on several occasions.

During the annual Day of Remembrance, around 10,000 people, war veterans, military personnel, Members of Parliament, and royalty attend the ceremony, the public lining the procession route along Whitehall. At the 2020 Remembrance Day, because of the lockdown restrictions no members of the public were in attendance, the Queen and prime minister leading a much smaller, scaled-down ceremony.

Towards the middle of Whitehall, north of the Cenotaph, the memorial to the women of the Second World War was unveiled by the Queen on 9 July 2005, the 60th anniversary of the end of the Second World War and two days after a series of co-ordinated terrorist attacks across London. In the attack suicide bombers killed fifty-two people and injured more than 700 who were travelling on the city's public transport.

Despite this horrific event it was believed fitting for the ceremony to take place, the unveiling followed by a fly past of military helicopters and aircraft all flown by female pilots and crew. Funded through a charitable trust, the memorial bronze, sculptured by John W. Mills, depicts seventeen sets of uniform and clothes symbolising the different work carried out by women throughout the war.

Ever since the reign of James II, when bishops arrived at Whitehall Palace to protest against being forced to read out the Declaration of Indulgence in church, which promoted broad religious freedom, Whitehall has been the scene of various incidents of public disorder. In 2015, after the Conservative Party won a majority in the general election, protestors sprayed red graffiti on the symbolic *Women of World War II* memorial.

To the south of Whitehall are the Houses of Parliament and Great George Street, which during the mid-1700s consisted of various yards and alleyways with at least three inns – the Antelope, the Boar's Head, and the George, sited at George Yard. After a series of alterations were made to the street layout, Great George Street first appears in the 1759 rate book, taking its name from the old inn.

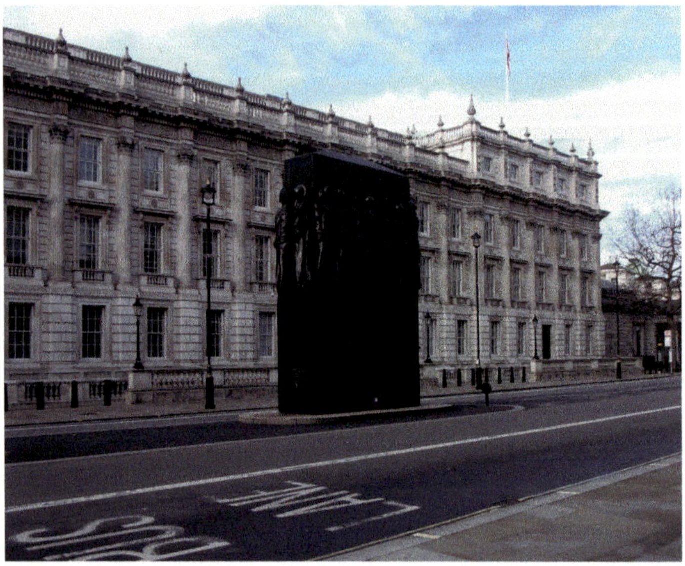

Women of World War Two, SW1.

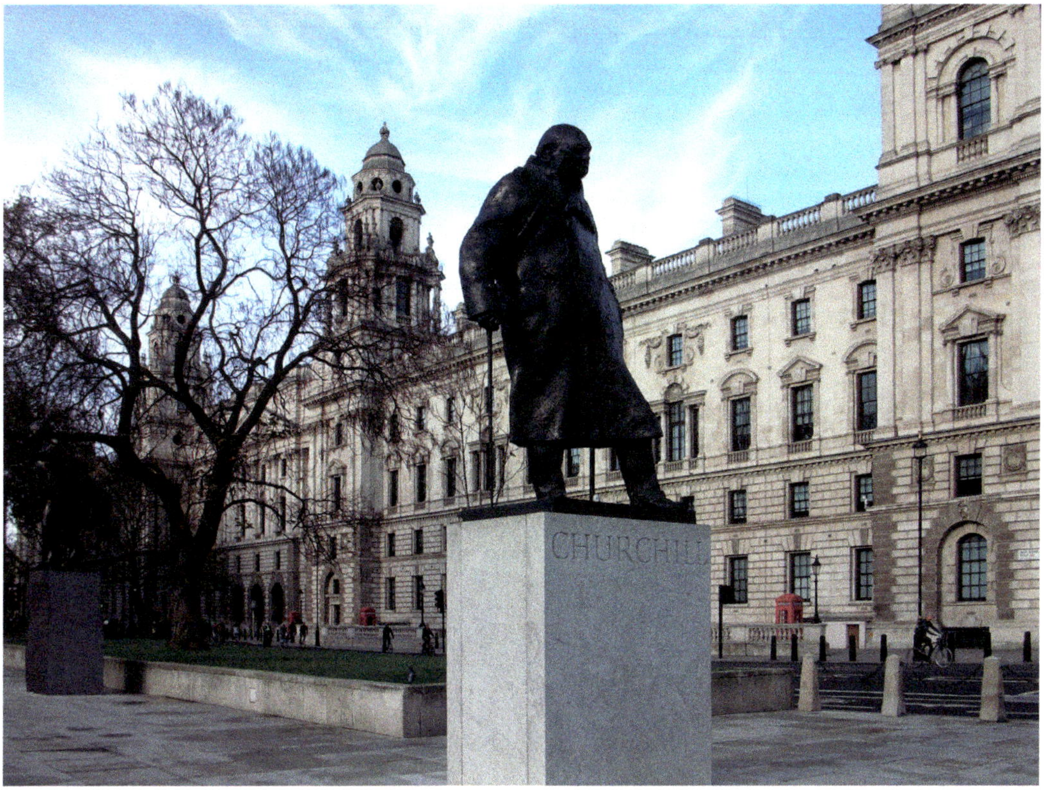

Great George Street, SW1.

During the early nineteenth century, properties to the east of the street were demolished as part of an improvement scheme authorised by an Act of Parliament, and in 1910 the buildings to the north were knocked down to make way for government offices.

To the south is Parliament Square and the bronze statue of former British Prime Minister Winston Churchill, sculptured by Ivor Robert Jones and unveiled in 1973. Like other memorials in the vicinity, Churchill's statue has also become a target for activists and has been defaced on many occasions during protests.

Laid out in 1868 to open out space around the Palace of Westminster, Parliament Square was constructed on the site of slum properties, demolished to make way for the busy traffic junction. Before the road changes, Westminster was a one of London's poor and densely crowded outer parishes, an independent district with its own liberties during the plague outbreak. Living in poorly maintained and unsanitary slums, for those who fell victim to the plague there was very little prospect of any medical care, as witnessed by Samuel Pepys, who wrote, 'In Westminster, there is never a physician or apothecary left, all being dead.' It has been estimated over 300 died from the epidemic in the parishes of Westminster. The victims were buried at Tothil Fields, the pits now below government buildings.

Among the tenements around Westminster Palace, a large seventeenth-century manor, Lindsay House, residence of the Earl of Abingdon, stood at the south-west end of Lindsay Lane, Abingdon Street.

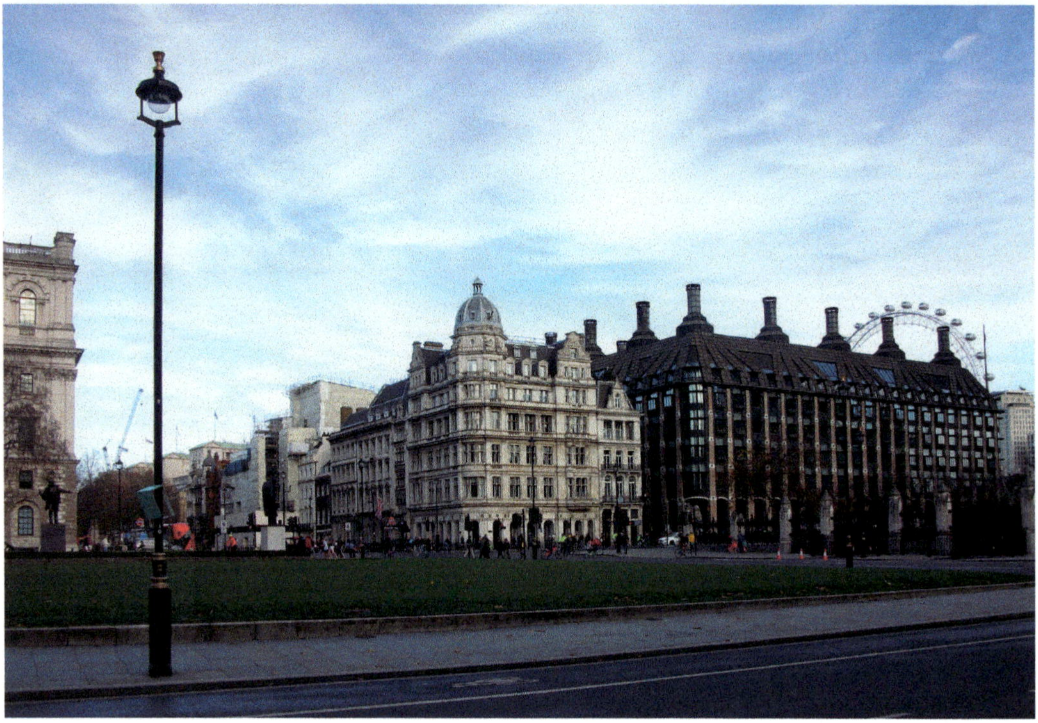

Parliament Square, SW1.

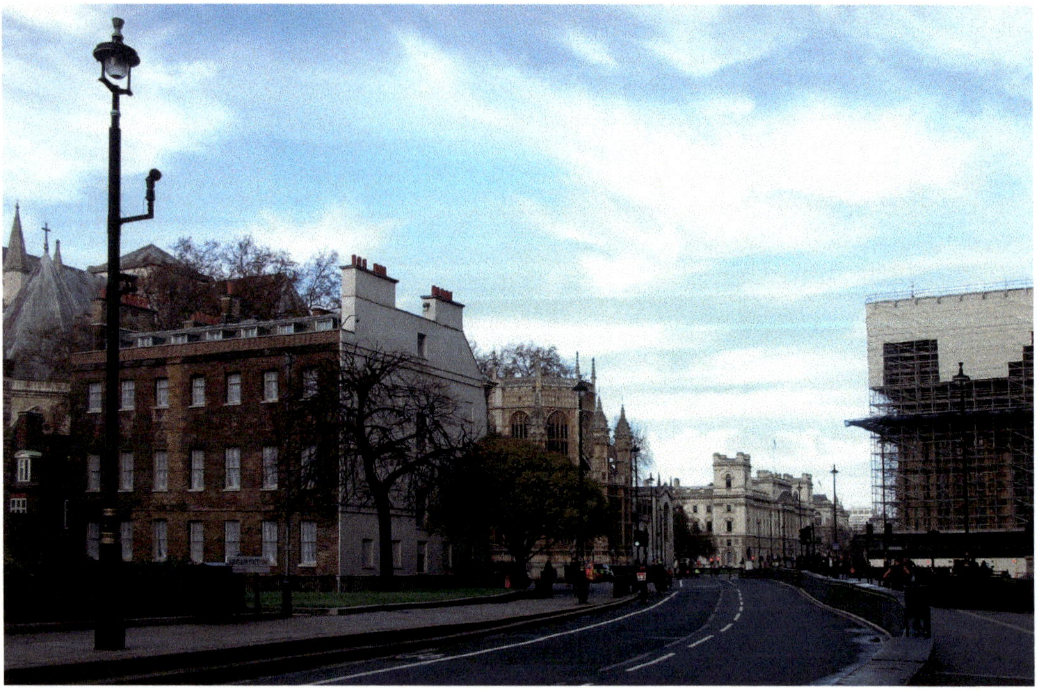

Abingdon Street, SW1.

Originally known as Lindsay Lane, after the manor, and then Dirty Lane, when the street was widened as part of the approach improvements to Westminster Bridge in 1750, the lane was renamed Abingdon Street. Of the houses that survived the road improvements all but a few were left standing after the Blitz, and when later demolished a medieval quay was discovered among the foundations.

An expanse of vacant land to the west of the street was developed into Abingdon Garden, directly opposite the barricades running the length of the street outside the Houses of Parliament, erected as protection against terrorist car bomb attacks.

To the south of the Houses of Parliament, overlooking Victoria Public Gardens, Victoria Tower was erected as a purpose-built fireproof repository for documents after a fire destroyed the medieval buildings and a majority of the House of Commons records in 1834.

In the public gardens at the foot of the tower is a bronze by Rodin, *The Burghers of Calais*, purchased by the government in 1911 and one of twelve original castings commemorating the siege of the French port in 1346. The sculpture depicts the six burghers who surrendered to Edward III, sparing the lives of the town's citizens.

Retaining its royal status for ceremonial purposes, the Palace of Westminster was struck by bombs on fourteen occasions during the Second World War. During one air raid the roof of Westminster caught fire and the Chamber of Commons was destroyed. Unlike

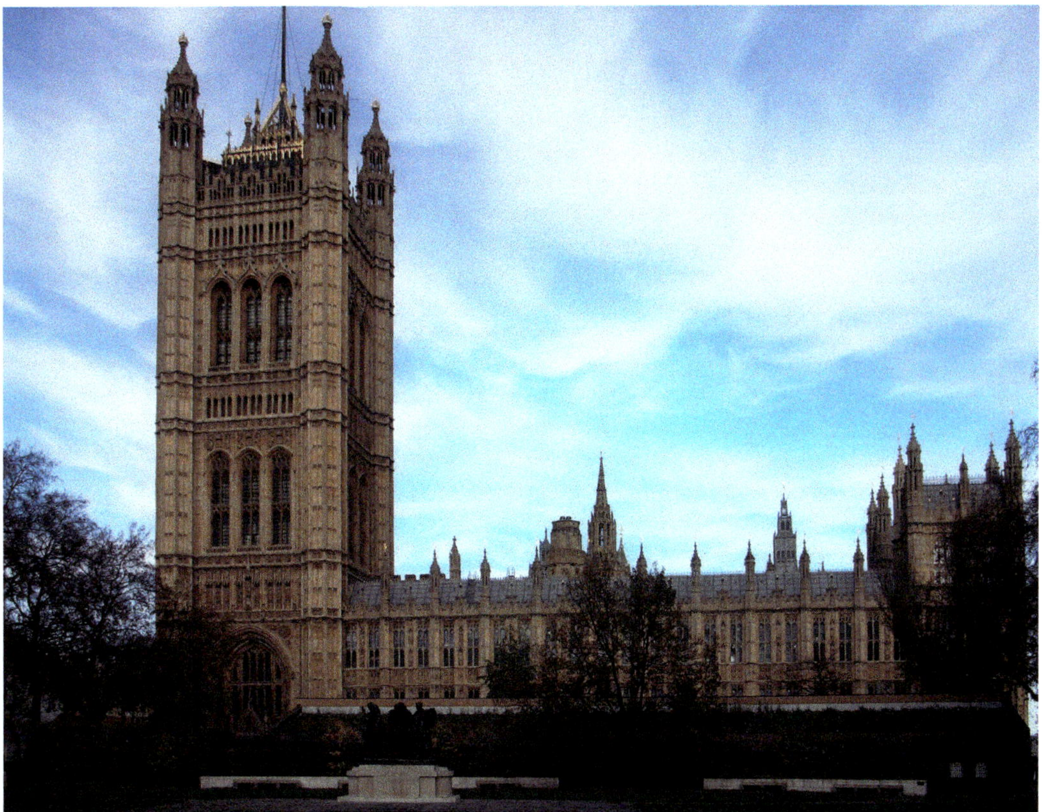

Victoria Tower Gardens, SW1.

times past, when Members of Parliament evacuated London during the plague, ministers remained in the capital, and from late June 1941 until October 1950 the Commons relocated to the Lords Chamber and the lords met in the Robing Room.

The embankment wall in Victoria Tower Gardens was breached during an air raid after a bomb exploded, leaving a wide gap almost 20 feet wide, the crater reaching down to the foreshore. To prevent flooding at high tide a sandbag barrier was built around the crater until permanent repairs were made.

Linking South West London to Lambeth, Westminster Bridge (completed in 1862) replaced the original stone bridge erected in 1736 to link a rapidly growing Westminster to the South Bank. The only way of crossing the river previously at this point was by the Archbishop of Canterbury's horse ferry or by boat – the Archbishop and watermen were financially compensated for loss of business when permission was given to build the original bridge.

By the eighteenth century, the South Bank had evolved into a large, industrial dockside community, and through migrants from outside the city and famine-stricken Ireland relocating here during the mid-1800s, the population of Lambeth grew to around 130,000 parishioners, living in hastily built tenements on the waterfront marshland with no sanitation or standing waterpipes. The only source of water for drinking and washing came from the polluted Thames. Unsurprisingly, in 1848 an epidemic of cholera broke out, killing around 1,600 people.

In the afternoon of 7 April 2017, six people lost their lives and fifty were injured in an act of terrorism when a car deliberately drove into pedestrians on Westminster Bridge before crashing into the perimeter fence of the Palace of Westminster. Following this attack barricades were installed at the road's edge, like other of the capital's road bridges, to prevent vehicles mounting the pavement.

During lockdown, Westminster was virtually free from traffic and pedestrians, and entertainment venues and attractions on the South Bank, the Royal Festival Hall, the London Eye, the London Dungeon, and the Sea Life Centre were closed temporarily.

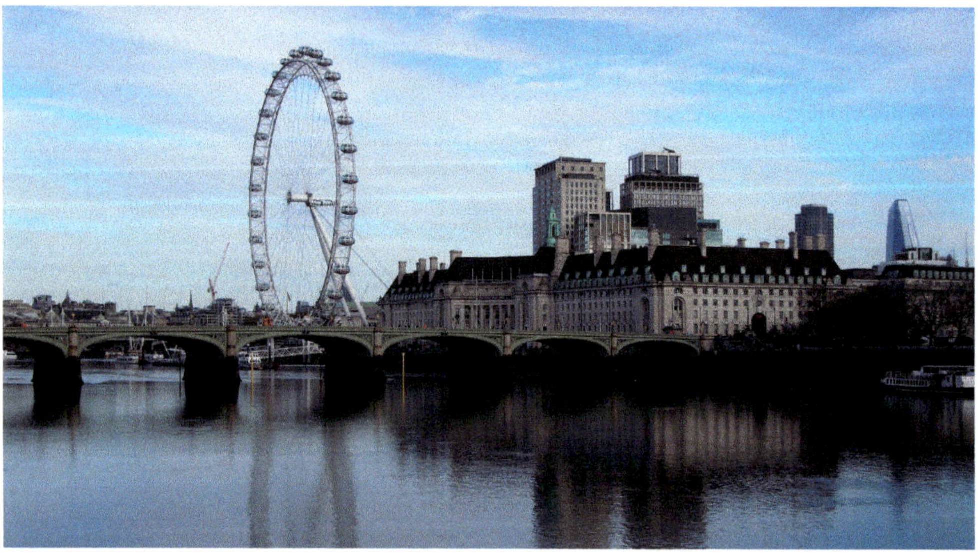

Westminster Bridge, SW1.

4

Expanding Boundaries

'All the towne almost going out of towne.'

Samuel Pepys (1665)

To escape the Great Plague, and then the Great Fire, many of London's wealthy fled to their country estates or to more affluent districts to the west of the city. It has been estimated between 15 and 20 per cent of London's population abandoned the city after the 1665 plague outbreak. A priest at the time, Simon Patrick, remarked it was the ordinary sort of people who remained, while the gentry were gone.

Throughout the early seventeenth century, as the population of the city grew, many country-style houses and manors were built on areas of undeveloped land and open spaces, which became known as London's West End.

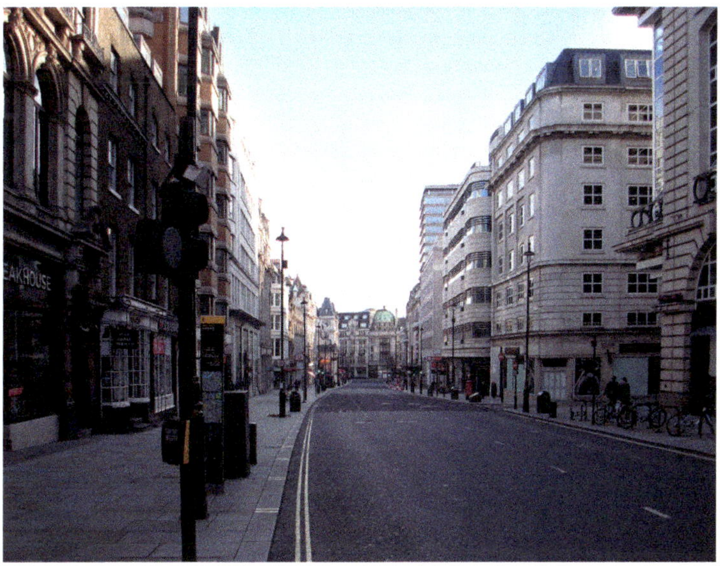

Haymarket, SW1.

Running south from Piccadilly Circus to Pall Mall, the Haymarket originated as a rural street market close to Charing village where fodder, straw, and hay was sold. Charles II granted rights to hold a twice-weekly market for selling sheep and cattle; however, within a few years the Haymarket had become so filthy that James I attempted to have it closed down. Although the sheep and cattle market moved to Regent's Park, hay and straw continued to be sold from the Haymarket up until 1830.

By this time the spacious Haymarket had been paved, and shops, inns and theatres had been erected each side, including the Queen's Theatre, the Theatre Royal and His Majesty's Theatre. On the north-east corner of Haymarket was a gentleman's gaming house, Shaver's Hall, attached to indoor tennis courts, once the headquarters of English tennis.

Well known for its musical instruments, book shops and the Garrick, Phoenix, and Wyndham theatres, Charing Cross Road was created through a widening of Crown Street and Castle Street, taking its name from a village close to the Thames, Charing, known in Old English as *Cierran*, meaning a bend in the river.

After Edward I's wife, Eleanor, died in 1290, the king commissioned twelve stone crosses to be made and then erected where the queen's funeral procession came to rest on its way to Westminster Abbey; the last cross was placed to the south of Trafalgar Square.

One of its many bookshops, Mark's & Co., featured in a publication written by Helen Halfe, *84, Charing Cross Road*. This usually busy road was empty of people and traffic from the closure of its theatres, restaurants and shops during lockdown.

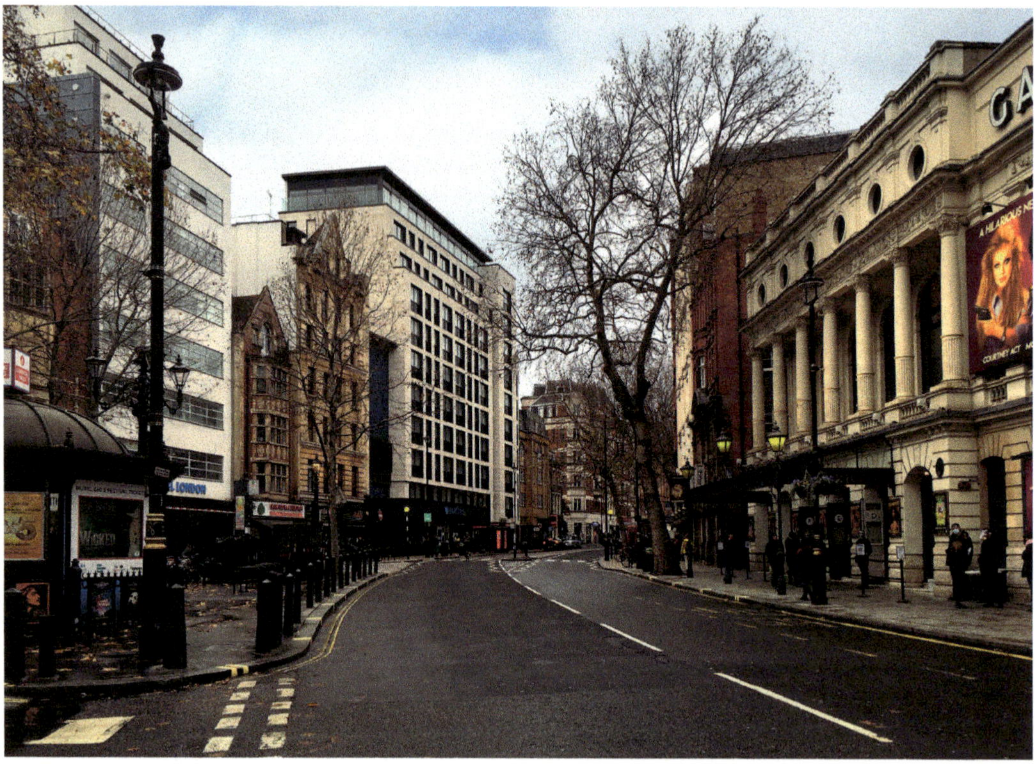

Charing Cross Road, WC2.

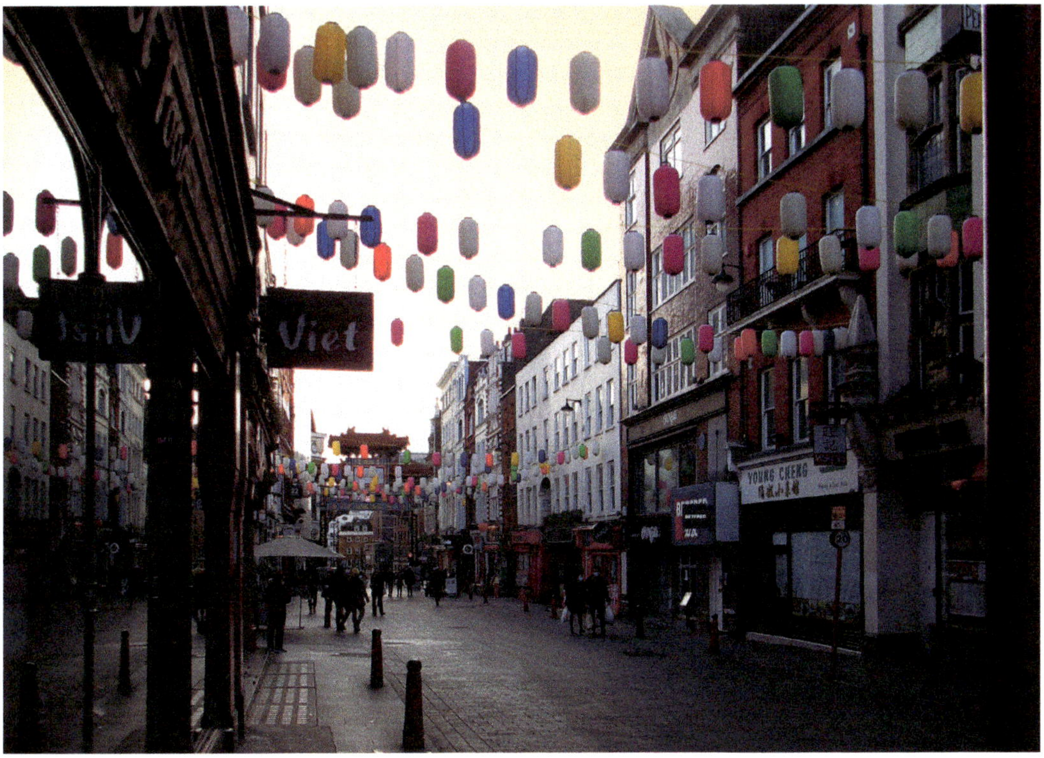

Gerrard Street, W1.

A large expanse of land owned by Lord Gerrard to the west of Charing Cross Road was used at one time as a military training ground. It was developed by Nicholas Barbon during the seventeenth century and properties were built for the gentry, who were moving away from the overpopulated parishes of the city.

By the mid-nineteenth century, Gerrard Street had become less well known for its elite residences and more acclaimed for its lively taverns and coffee houses frequented by a diversity of artists and writers. In the 1970s, the Chinese community, largely based in Limehouse, East London, relocated to the West End, opening markets, shops, restaurants, and businesses, transforming the neglected district into the colourful and vibrant Chinatown.

Gerrard Street runs through one of London's most important centres of the hospitality trade. The lively and atmospheric independently run restaurants, once busy all through the week, suffered more than many others during lockdown. Although the government's 'Eat Out to Help Out' scheme assisted the hospitality sector financially, many Chinatown restaurants are on the brink of permanent closure through loss of income.

To the south of Chinatown, Leicester Square is the main location for London's film premieres, where large crowds gather to cheer the arrival of stars from the silver screen. It also hosted the annual London Film Festival before cinemas closed during lockdown. The European premiere of Disney's *Mulan* at the Odeon fell victim to the pandemic restrictions. During the Middle Ages, the land now occupied by Leicester Square was divided between the Beaumont family and the Abbot of St Peter's Westminster Abbey.

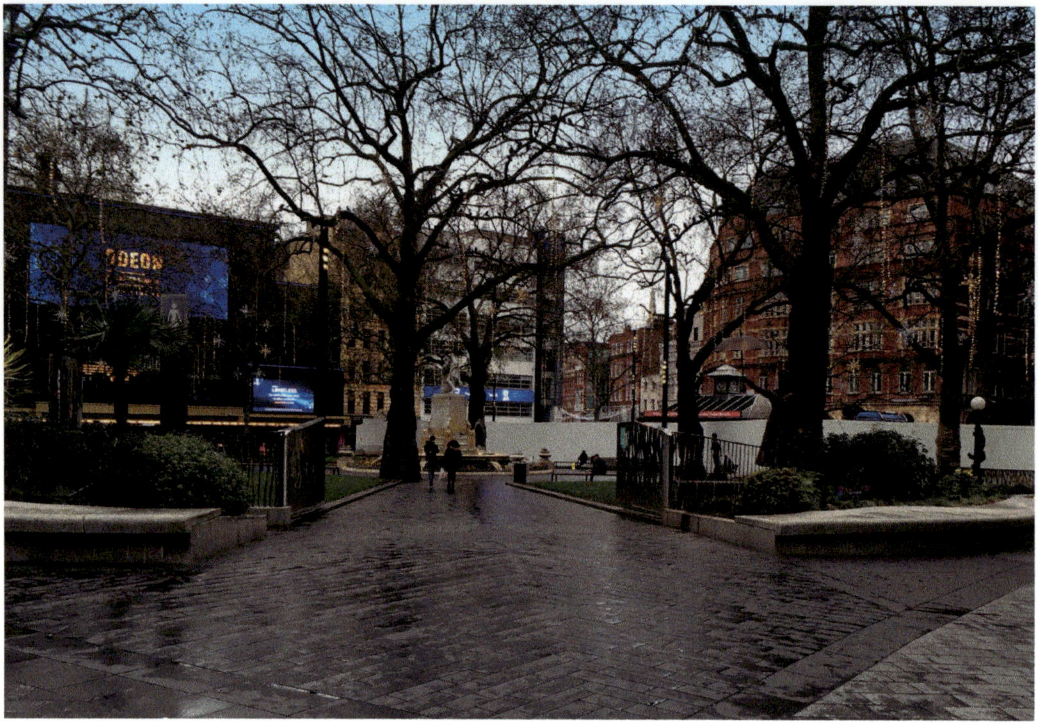

Leicester Square, WC2.

After the death of Lord Beaumont's widow, the land (mostly fields) was acquired by Henry VIII, having already taking the abbot's share, surrendered through the Dissolution of the Monasteries. By the mid-seventeenth century, the 2nd Earl of Leicester erected one of London's largest houses to the north of the open square, away from the poorer districts afflicted by outbreaks of the plague. Elegant, tall, residential properties were then erected along the remaining three sides of the square, and although at first no shops were allowed, the 3rd Earl of Leicester gave permission for booths to be erected in front of Leicester House.

Demolished in the late 1700s, the house was replaced by buildings with shops and retail outlets, and on the other three sides were a variety of houses with shops, a music hall, theatre, cinema, public house and hotel, the square becoming a centre of entertainment. The middle of the square was originally used as common land for herding cattle before being transformed into a park during the late 1800s, where today visitors can spot bronze statues of film characters situated in and around the gardens.

Another of London's most popular tourist attractions, Piccadilly Circus, built during the early 1800s to connect Regent Street with Piccadilly, was once surrounded by a multitude of illuminated advertising boards fixed to the outside of the buildings. Although there are now fewer illuminations to see, Piccadilly Circus is still an extremely popular and vibrant place to visit, with bustling crowds navigating their way across the exceedingly busy road junctions and around the Shaftesbury Memorial Fountain.

Erected in 1893 to commemorate philanthropist Anthony Ashley-Cooper, the 7th Earl of Shaftesbury, the fountain once stood at the centre of the junction before being relocated

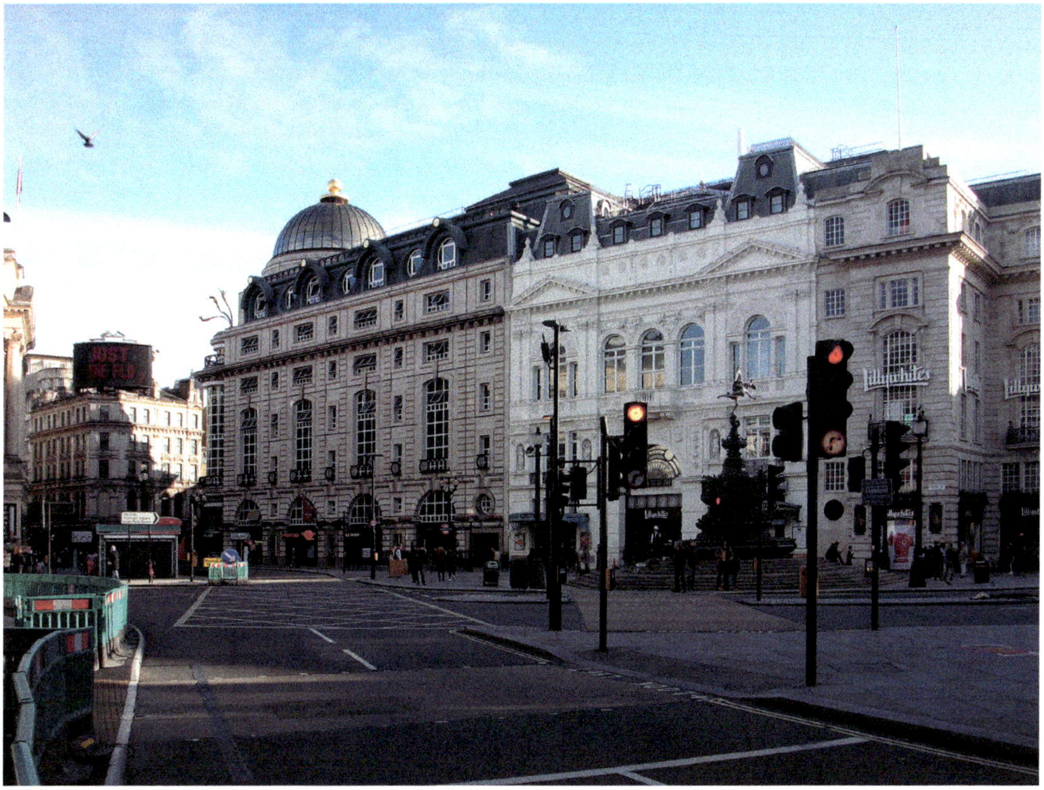

Piccadilly Circus, W1.

to its present site in the late 1980s. The statue of a winged archer, commonly referred to as Eros, is a representation of his brother Anteros, the angel of Christian charity, the first London statue cast in aluminium.

At the outbreak of the Second World War, the memorial was boarded up and the statue removed for safekeeping for fear of damage during bombing raids. Surviving the war, the memorial has been a target of several Irish republican terrorist attacks, and became a rallying point for various political demonstrations.

Shaftesbury Avenue was built towards the late 1800s as part of the slum clearances to provide a main thoroughfare through the crowded neighbourhoods of Soho and St Giles. During the time of the plague and Great Fire the district was sparsely populated, with a few houses scattered among fields and meadows.

To the north of Shaftesbury Avenue, Soho evolved from farmland into a royal park, which, after the last plague outbreak, developed into a fashionable district for the aristocracy. By the mid-1800s most of the gentry had moved out and Soho, overcrowded with people living in wretched conditions, suffered a severe outbreak of cholera. By the early 1900s, Soho then became the centre of London's salubrious red-light district, notorious for its nightclubs and strip joints.

At the junction of Shaftesbury Avenue and Piccadilly Circus, one of London's ancient main roads leading west was believed to have been named Piccadilly after a fashionable

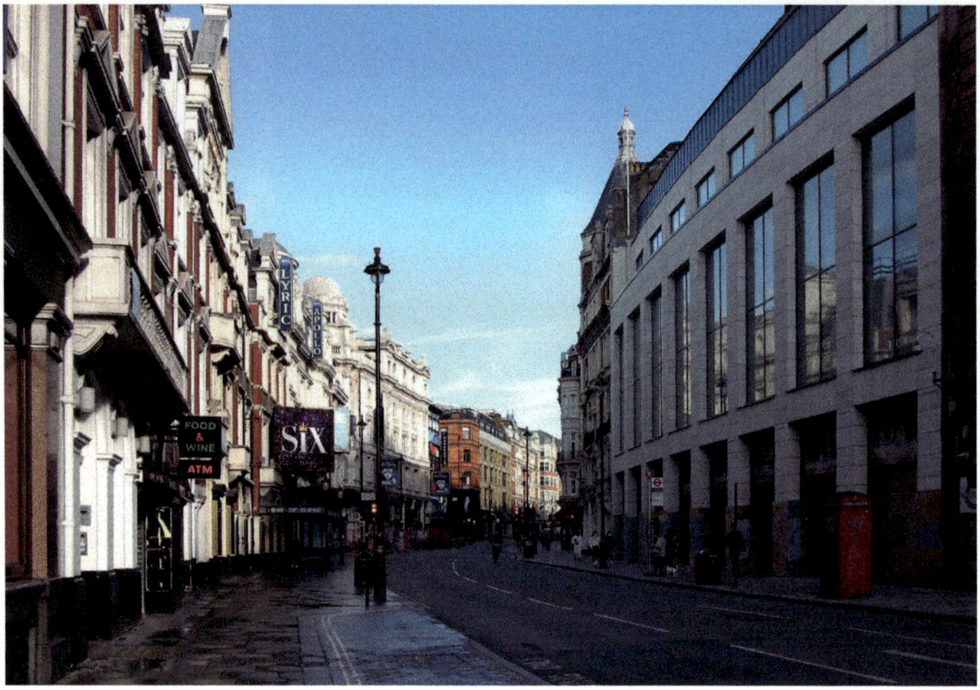

Shaftesbury Avenue, W1.

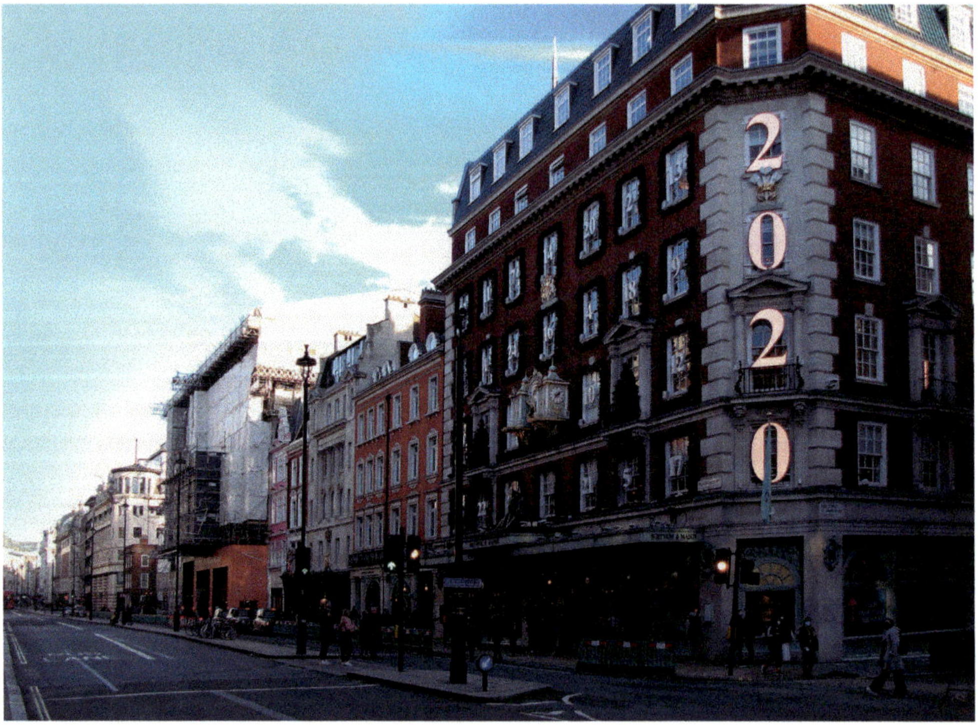

Piccadilly, W1.

seventeenth-century stiff collar worn at court – a 'picadil'. The tailor who sold the picadils, Robert Baker, was said to have made so much money from sales that he purchased land north of the road, where he built Piccadilly Hall.

When land to the west of Piccadilly Circus reverted to the crown, the thoroughfare was named Portugal Street, after Charles I's Portuguese-born wife Catherine of Braganza.

Following the Restoration, Charles II encouraged the development of the street and the district of Mayfair to the north, where many grand mansions were built. By the early 1700s, most of these properties were demolished and replaced by more fashionable buildings, and the street was renamed Piccadilly. It was renowned for its many inns, gentlemen's clubs and Fortnum & Mason store, which sold fresh and dried fruit, poultry, lobsters, and savoury foods to the gentry.

The development of Mayfair and St James's made Piccadilly one of the busiest thoroughfares in London.

To link High Holborn directly to Oxford Street a new thoroughfare was completed in 1847, which drove directly through the slum area of St Giles. During the nineteenth century, many road remodelling schemes were used as a means to demolish the lawless and poverty-stricken areas surrounding the more prosperous districts of London.

Named New Oxford Street, it became a popular place for students from the newly established London University to shop for books and pamphlets at many of the street's booksellers. Running to the south of Bloomsbury, New Oxford Street joined Oxford Street at the busy crossroad junction of Tottenham Court Road and Charing Cross Road.

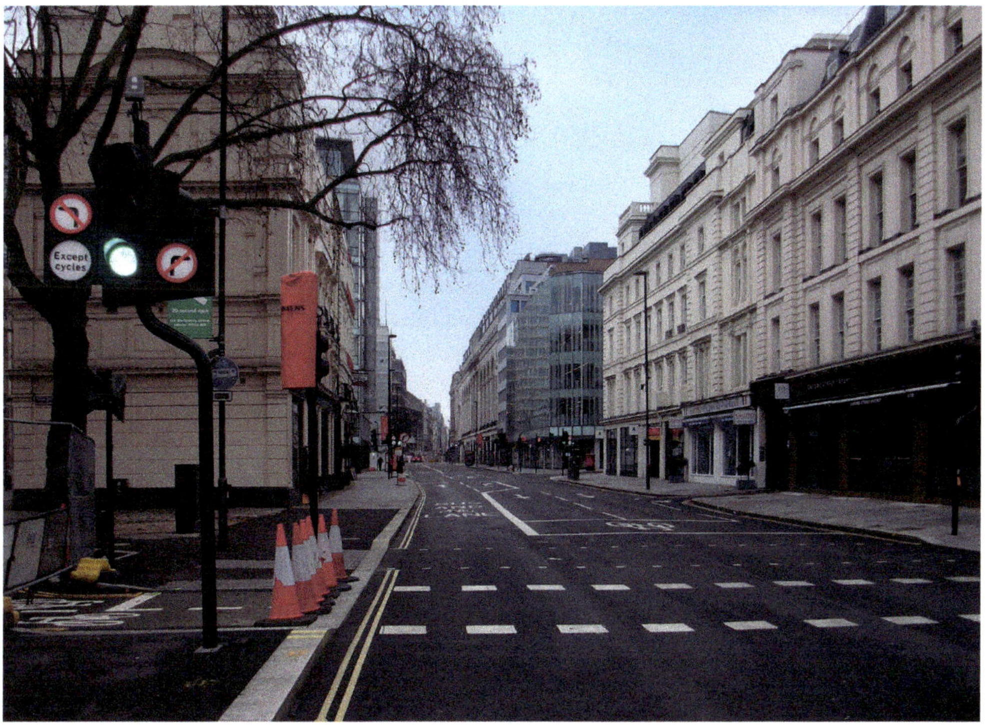

New Oxford Street, WC1.

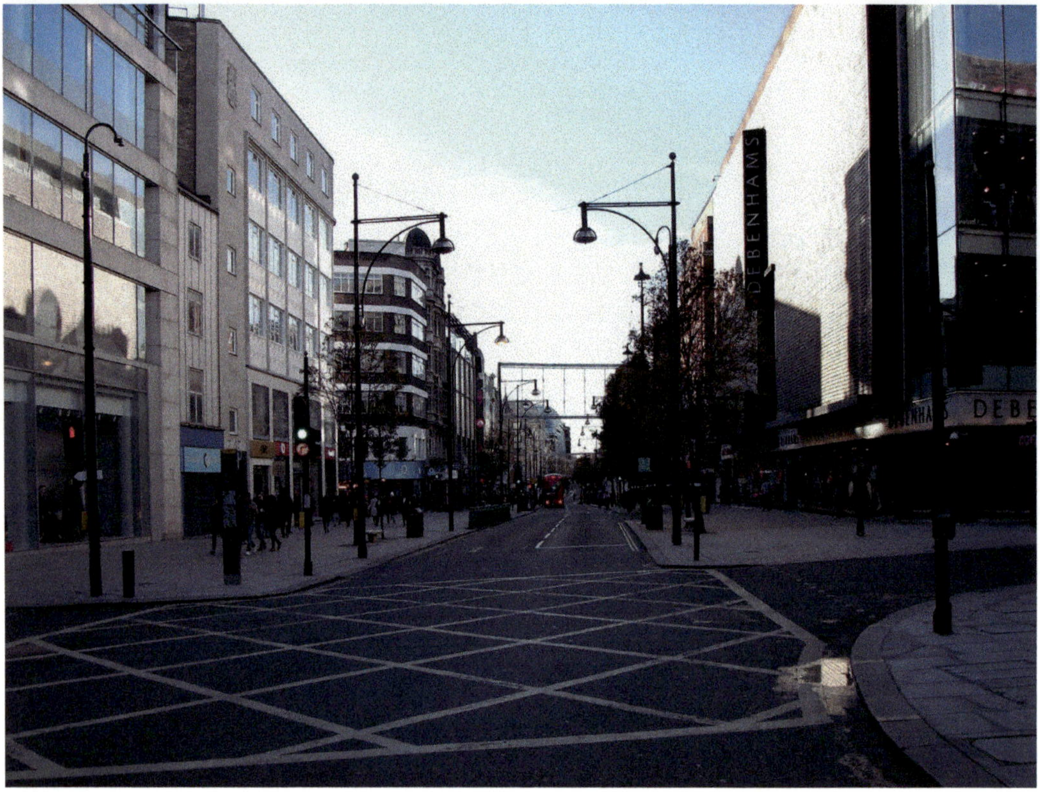

Oxford Street, W1.

The old Roman road out of London to Oxford was once referred to as 'the Tyburn Way', after the Tyburn stream flowing close by at Bond Street, a route used to transport condemned prisoners to Tyburn Gallows at Marble Arch. The name Oxford Street has been used since the eighteenth century, after the 2nd Earl of Oxford acquired land through marriage to the north of the thoroughfare. The street then evolved into a popular place for the wealthy residing at Marylebone and Mayfair to shop, where traders dealt mostly in drapery and fine furnishings. By the early nineteenth century, a variety of other retailers moved onto the street. London's first department store, Selfridges, opened its headquarters at the west end of Oxford Street in 1910.

Renowned for its brightly lit street decorations over the festive period, an estimated 0.5 million people visit Oxford Street every day. Many of the buildings along the popular shopping street were damaged by bombing during the Second World War, and Selfridges, along with many London department stores, has been targeted by terrorist bombers.

Although surviving past catastrophise and tragedies, during the pandemic as a result of lockdown restrictions and a lack of tourism Oxford Street became a shadow of its former self.

According to Bloomberg, with footfall down by an estimated 59 per cent since 2019, the New West End Company, representing businesses located at Oxford Street, Regent Street and Bond Street, forecast a drop in annual sales up to March 2021, from £10 billion

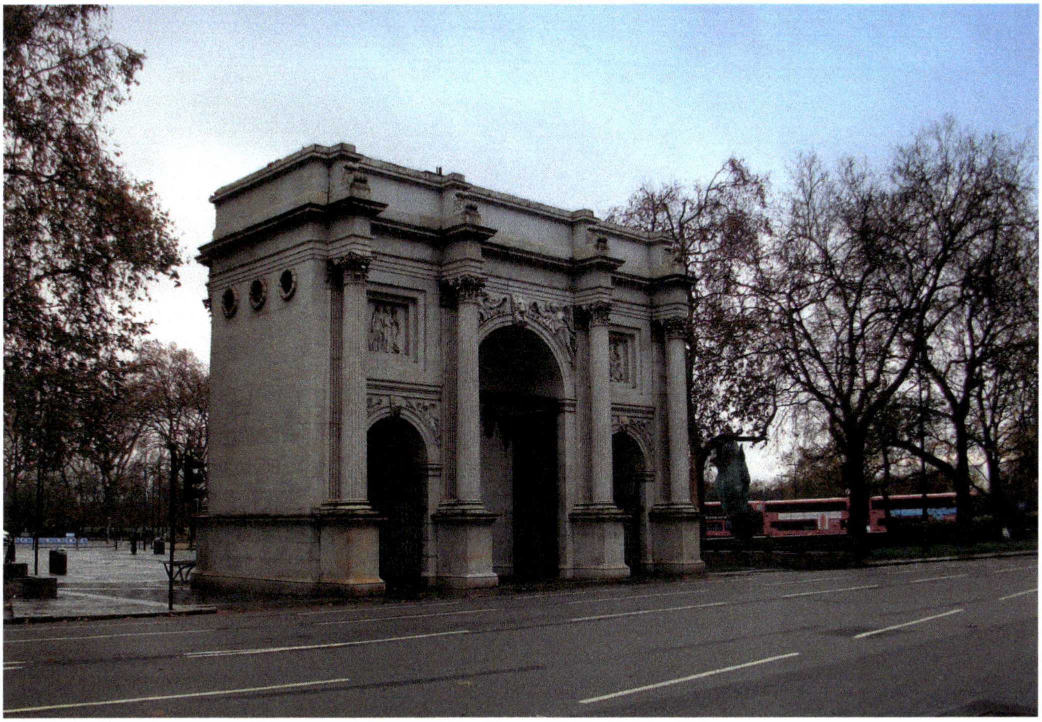

Marble Arch, W1.

the previous year to £2 billion. Shaftesbury PLC, which owns 600 properties in the area, including shops, restaurants, and bars, wrote down the value of its estate by £700 million.

To the west of Oxford Street is one of central London's busiest road junctions, Marble Arch, where up until lockdown the average annual traffic flow totalled an estimated 9,427 vehicles each day.

Intended to be the state entrance to Buckingham Palace, Marble Arch was relocated to the north-east corner of Hyde Park in 1851, when plans were made to enlarge the palace. Designed by John Nash, the arch was faced with white Carrara marble from Tuscany. When Park Lane was widened to improve traffic flow, Marble Arch was islanded with gardens, accessed by several pedestrian road crossings. At one time, only members of the Royal Family or King's Troop, Royal Artillery were permitted to pass through the main gated entrance of the arch.

Situated at the west end of Oxford Street, Bond Street is one of London's most exclusive shopping streets, created by Sir Thomas Bond on fields surrounding Clarendon House. Built in two stages from Piccadilly northwards to Oxford Street, by the mid-1700s Bond Street had become a popular place for aristocrats from Mayfair to shop and socialise.

The upper part became known as New Bond Street and the lower section, Old Bond Street. Many of the shopkeepers let the upper floors of their properties to notable residents such as William Pitt the Elder, Lord Nelson, Jonathan Swift, and James Boswell.

By the nineteenth century, Bond Street's fashionable retailers included jewellers, silversmiths and goldsmiths, various clothes outfitters, exclusive confectioners, tobacconists,

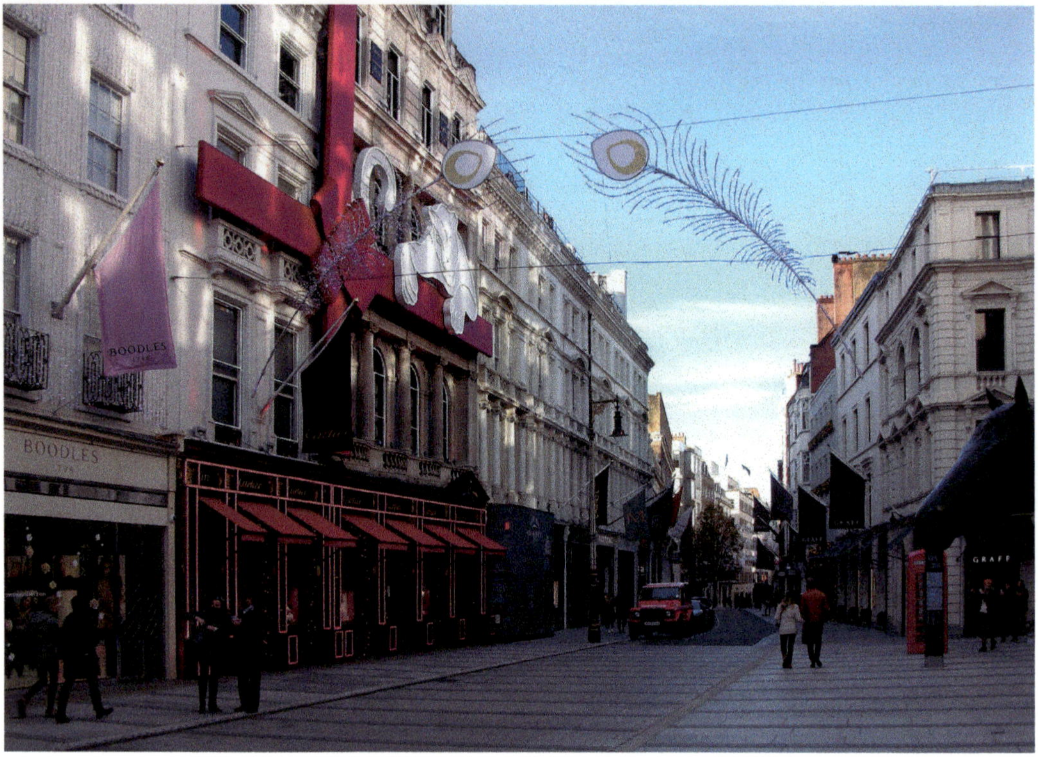

New Bond Street, W1.

and shoemakers, as well as Sotheby's auctioneers. Midway along New Bond Street is a statue of Winston Churchill and Franklin D. Roosevelt sitting on a wooden bench.

The bronze by Lawrence Holofcener – *Allies* – was unveiled in May 1995 to commemorate the 50th anniversary of the end of the Second World War. The bronze was positioned close to where New Bond Street was badly damaged by high-explosive bombs during the war. The ruined buildings were replaced in 1952 by the modernist Time and Life Building, decorated with a Henry Moore concrete sculpture.

London's most exclusive shopping arcade, running between Burlington Gardens and Piccadilly, was created in 1819 for Lord Caverndish of Burlington House, reputedly built to prevent people throwing rubbish and oyster shells into his garden. On completion, Burlington Arcade was occupied by sellers of jewellery and fancy goods, where ladies and gentlemen were able to shop in safety away from the dirty, crime-ridden streets of London. The arcade was raised in height when acquired by the Chesham family, and later sold to the Prudential Assurance Company in 1926.

The elegant, covered shopping arcade is patrolled by beadles, originally former soldiers of Lord Chesham's regiment, the 10th Hussars, to ensure the rules of the arcade are maintained by the public, which includes no singing, running, or whistling while shopping. It is believed the 'no whistling' regulation dates back to a time when prostitutes plied their trade in the arcade's upper rooms, the ladies of the night whistling a tuneful song as a warning when a beadle was about.

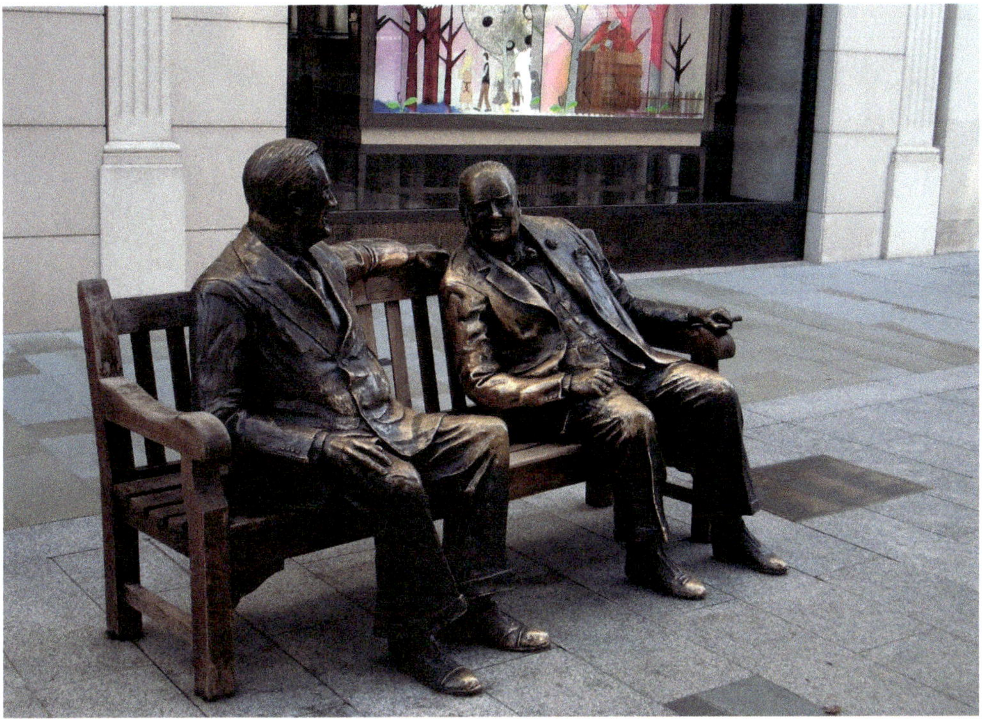

Allies, W1.

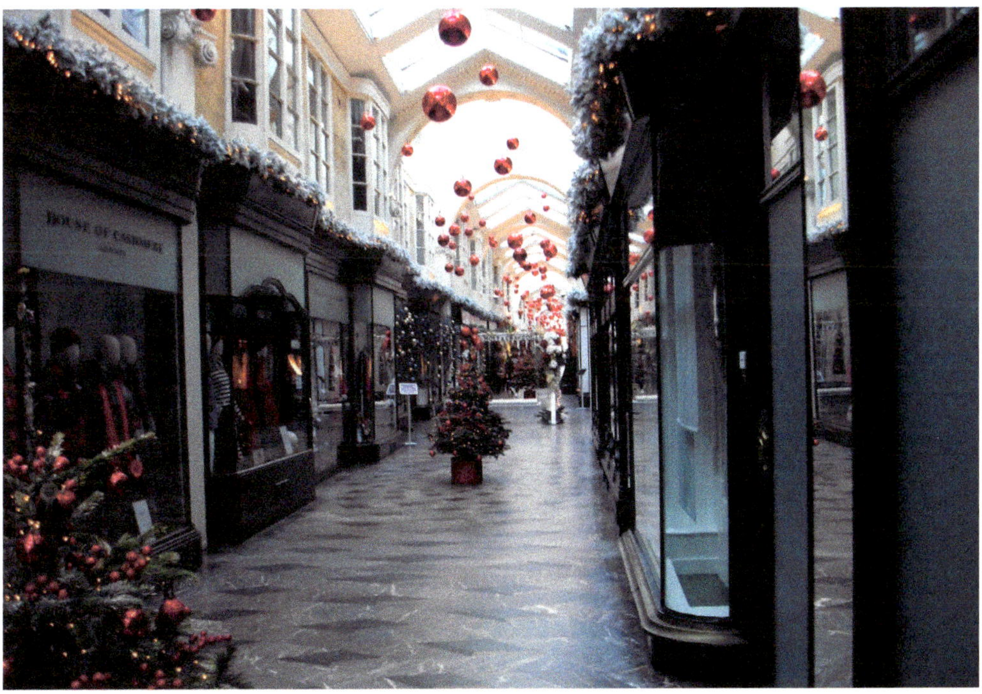

Burlington Arcade, W1.

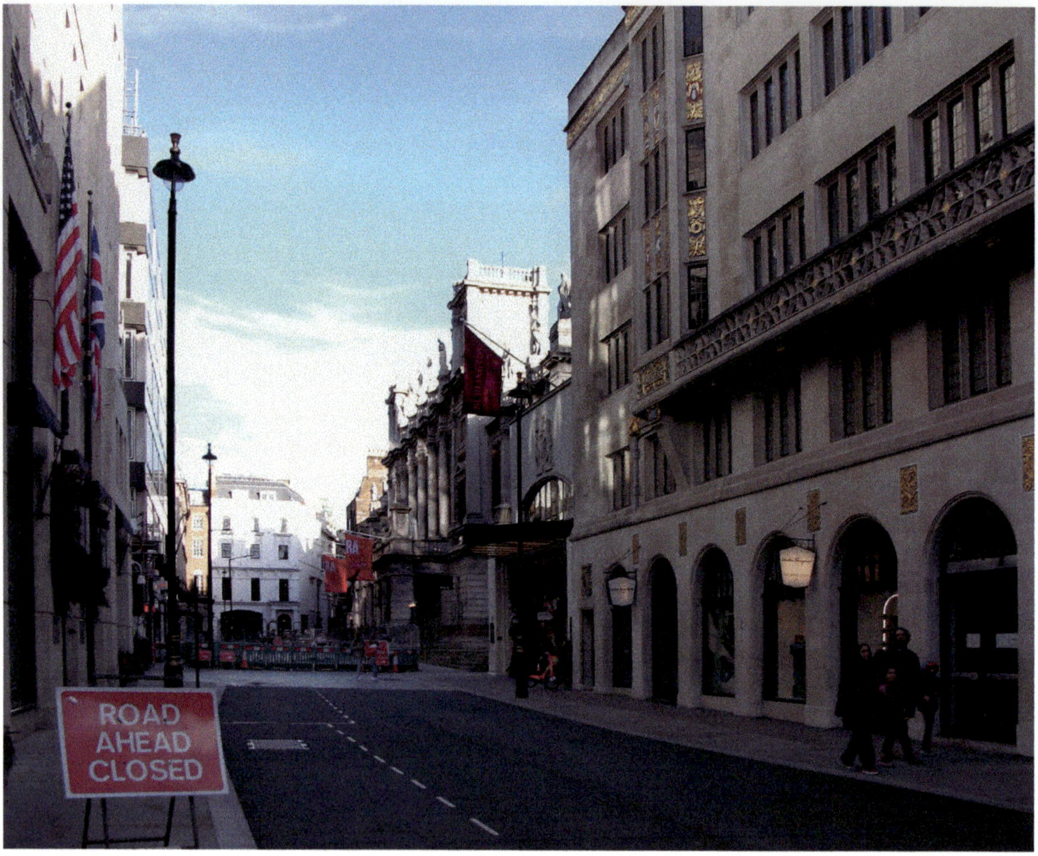

Burlington Gardens, W1.

As part of the Burlington estate, the gardens, originally an area of Glasshouse Street, extended from New Bond Street to Savile Row, bordering fields north of Piccadilly. Glasshouse Street appeared in 1678 rate books, the name possibly associated with resident potters supplying stoneware to the Glass Sellers' Company. Before the formation of Regent Street, the west end of the thoroughfare was renamed Burlington Gardens, the section between Bond Street and Savile Row becoming known as Vigo Lane.

Savile Row took its name from Lady Dorothy Savile, wife of the 3rd Earl of Burlington, and from the mid-1800s became celebrated for its tailors supplying made-to-measure clothes to the rich and famous. Burlington Gardens runs along the back of Burlington House, one of the earliest of many large private properties built on Piccadilly, now occupied by several eminent societies, including the Royal Academy of Arts.

London's most exclusive main road, Park Lane, to the west of Mayfair, was nothing more than a farm track up until the late 1700s, making up the eastern boundary of Hyde Park. When extensively used by coaches, the Kensington Turnpike Trust took over the lane's maintenance and several impressive large houses were then erected along the route. By the mid-1800s, Park Lane became a much sought-after place to live.

Many properties on Park Lane were either rebuilt or redeveloped, providing prestigious penthouse apartments alongside several exclusive hotels overlooking Hyde Park. Suffering

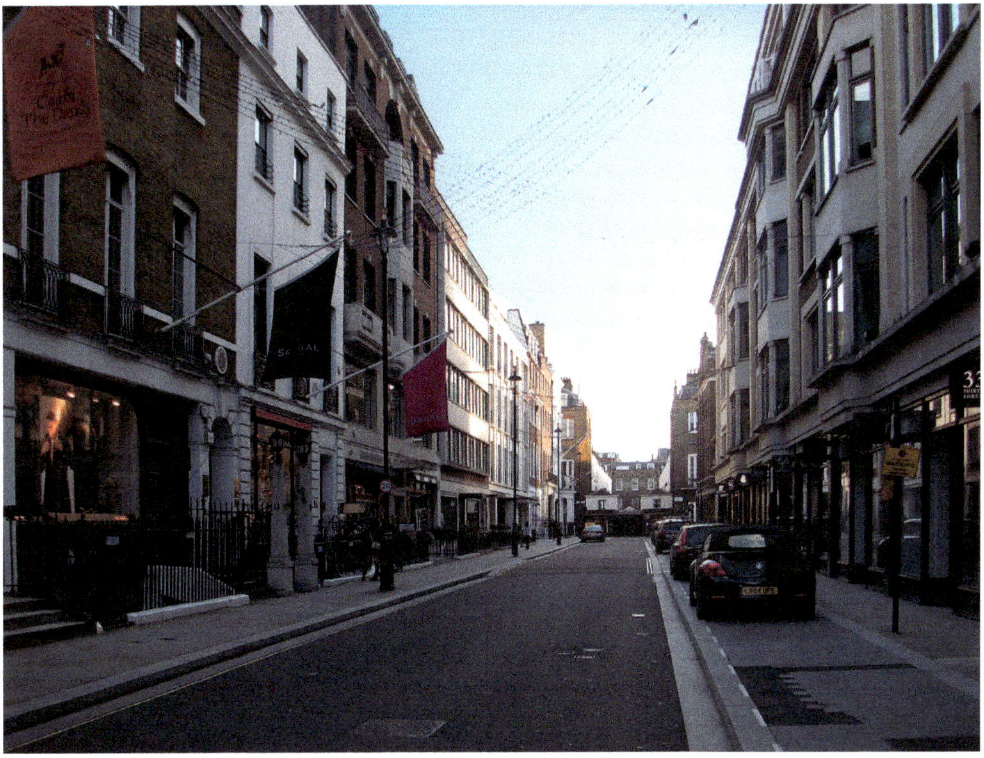

Savile Row, W1.

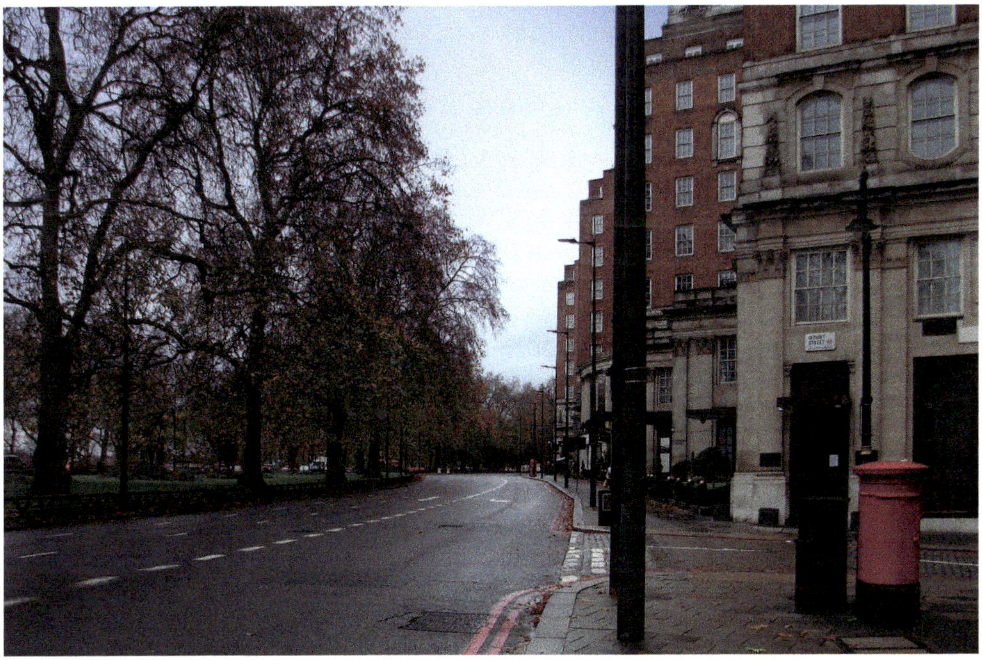

Park Lane, W1.

from traffic congestion since its creation in the mid-nineteenth century, several road improvements were made to Park Lane to improve traffic flow. Even with these road improvements, up until lockdown the dual carriageway was extremely busy throughout the week. Despite the high volume of vehicles passing daily, the properties on Park Lane continue to command some of the highest prices in London.

At the time of the Great Plague, Hyde Park Corner, at the southern end of Park Lane, was at the very edge of an ever-encroaching urbanisation, the open space separating London from the small communities of Kensington and Knightsbridge. The Hyde Park Corner toll gate was one of the busiest in London and remained in use up until 1825. Apsley House, the residence of the Duke of Wellington, was known as No. 1 London – the first house on the London side of the toll gate.

After road improvements were made to Hyde Park Corner during the early 1800s, an arch, intended as an outer entrance to Buckingham Palace, was erected as the centrepiece of the junction. Designed by Decimus Bruton and modelled on the Arch of Titus in Rome,

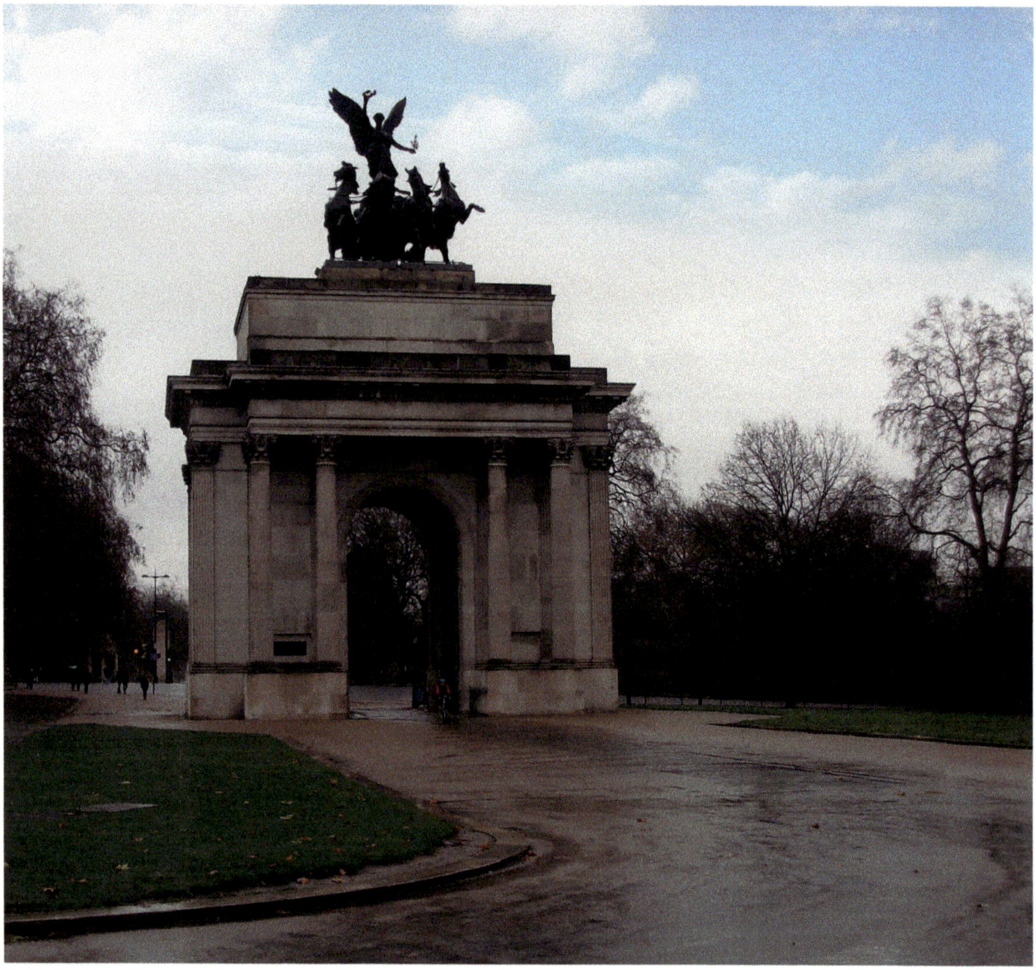

Wellington Arch, SW1.

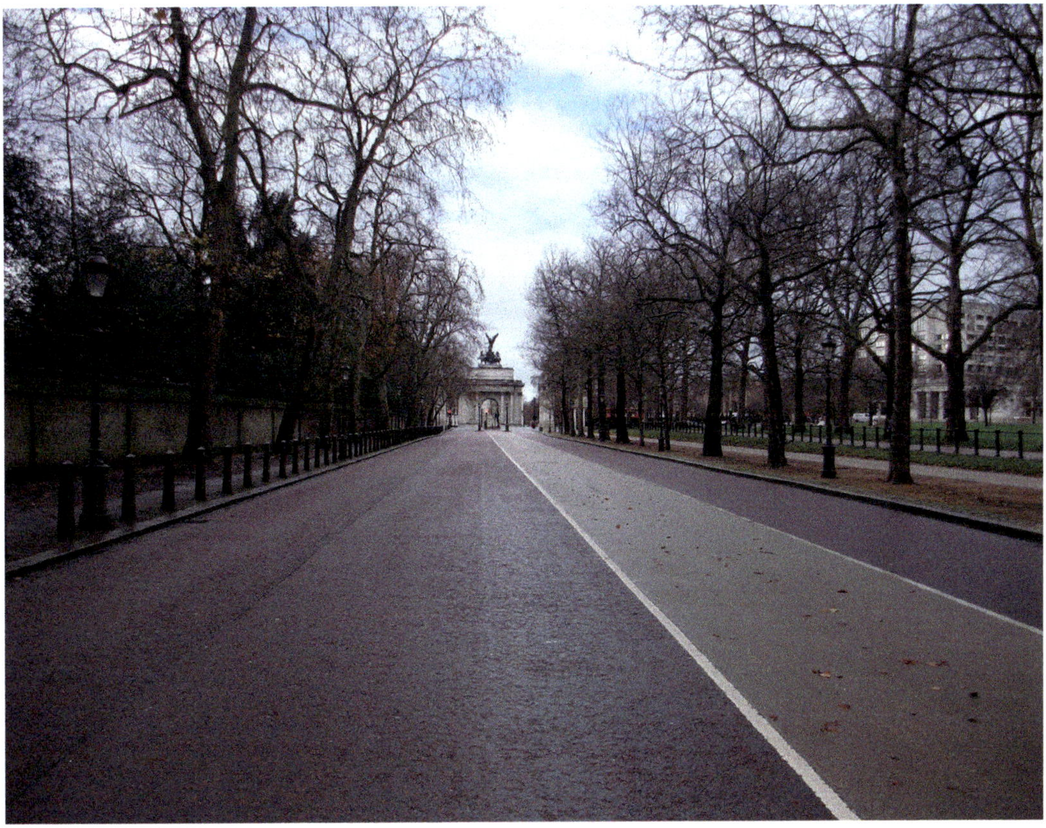

Constitution Hill, SW1.

the arch was named after the Duke of Wellington to commemorate British victories during the Napoleonic Wars.

Lacking any decorative sculptures on completion, the government commissioned a huge bronze equestrian statue of the duke to be mounted on top of the arch. The ungainly statue, erected in 1846, was considered out of proportion to the arch and received harsh criticism from the art world.

When the arch was relocated to the top of Constitution Hill to allow further widening of the junction, Wellington's statue was removed and a new statue, the Quadriga, the largest bronze statue cast in Europe, was erected in its place.

Built as a hollow structure, the arch once contained a small police station, and when ownership transferred to English Heritage the arch was opened to the public, where a Waterloo exhibition is displayed over three floors inside.

From the Wellington Arch, Constitution Hill runs eastwards between St James's Park and Buckingham Palace Gardens to the Victoria Memorial at the south end of The Mall. Usually busy with traffic, Constitution Hill began as a trackway known as Kings Coach to Kensington which ran through the middle of St James's Park.

Renamed Constitution Hill, it is believed the name refers to the constitutional walks Charles II took through the park. A popular place for duels, it was also the scene of three unsuccessful assassination attempts made on the life of Queen Victoria when travelling by carriage along the processional route from Buckingham Palace.

In 1850, after visiting the palace, Sir Robert Peel, founder of London's police force, was thrown from his horse and fatally injured when travelling through a gate on Constitution Hill into the park. At the eastern end the hill is accessed through the Commonwealth Memorial Gates, commemorating the armed forces of the British Empire, inaugurated by Elizabeth II during the Queen's Golden Jubilee year in 2002.

After the Great Fire and the rebuilding of the City of London, many open spaces away from the poorer districts of Westminster would soon come under development. Many large mansions and manors were built for the middling to upper social orders and members of the nobility.

One of the new, exclusive properties, Buckingham House, was built for the Duke of Buckingham in 1706 at the site of Arlington House. Acquired by George III in 1761, as a private residence for Queen Charlotte, Buckingham House was extensively remodelled and enlarged by architect John Nash, responsible for much of the layout of Regency London.

After Whitehall Palace burned down there were proposals to convert Buckingham Palace, as it had then become known, into the new Houses of Parliament. On the accession of Queen Victoria in 1837, Buckingham Palace became the monarch's main London residence. One of the most popular tourist landmarks, thousands would normally gather outside the palace waiting for the changing of the guard.

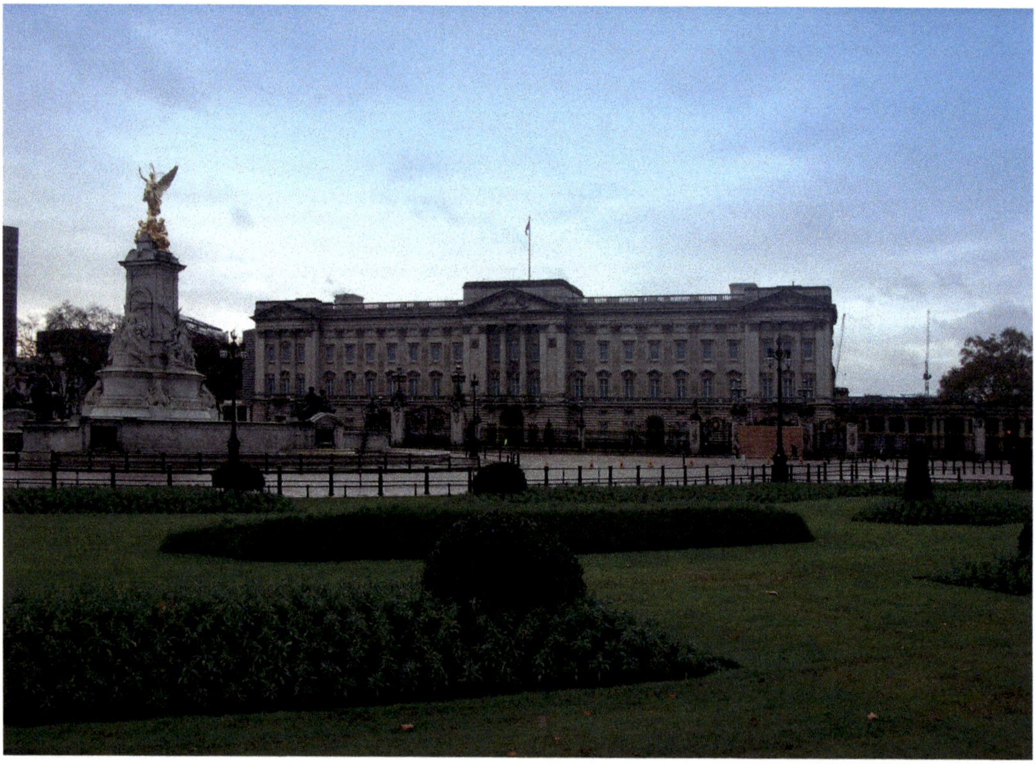

Buckingham Palace, SW1.

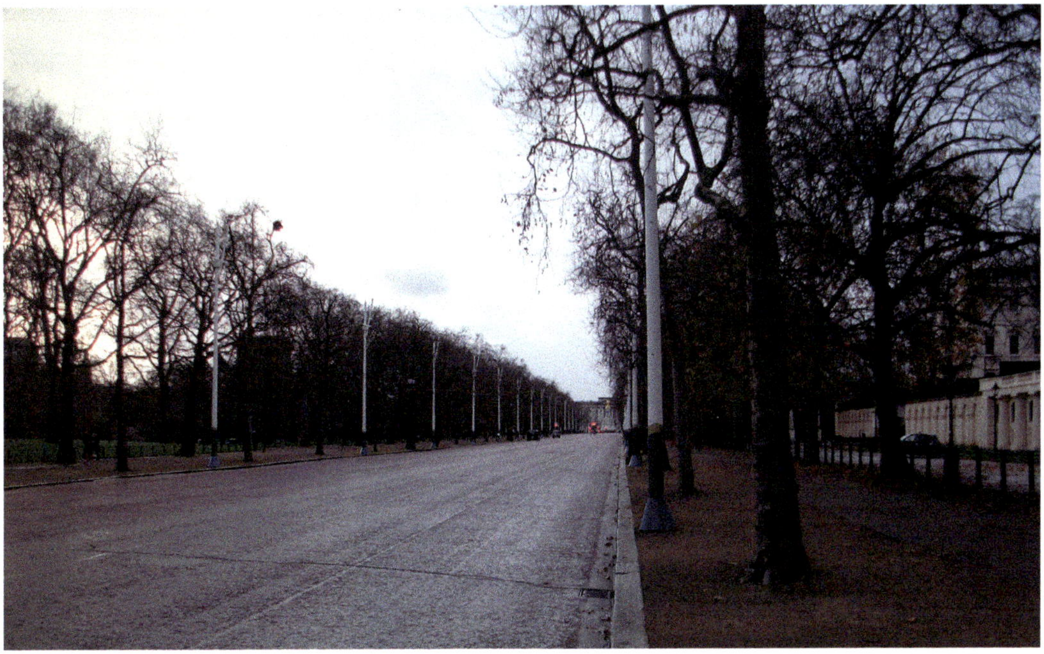

The Mall, SW1.

Thousands of people would also turn out on The Mall, a route from Buckingham Palace towards Trafalgar Square, in celebration of royal occasions – births, marriages, and coronations – along with military parades and state ceremonies. More recently, onlookers had the opportunity to cheer on athletes competing annual sporting events up until all public sporting pursuits and events were cancelled as a measure to stop the spread of the Covid-19 virus. The origin of The Mall came from the sporting ball game Pall-Mall, played on the strip of grassland during the mid-1700s, believed to have been introduced from France by James I.

The Mall became a fashionable social promenade bordered by tall trees, where people dressed in their finery would take a stroll every day to engage in conversations and discuss the news of the day. Planned as a ceremonial route in the early 1900s, The Mall was widened and the road surface coloured red to give the effect of a red carpet leading to Buckingham Palace.

Towards the Admiralty Arch end of The Mall, a majestic three-tier flight of steps lead to Waterloo Place, named in honour of the Duke of Wellington's victory over Napoleon at the Battle of Waterloo in 1815. The steps and Duke of York Column were completed in 1833 and the monument was dedicated to the second son of George III, Prince Frederick, Duke of York. As commander-in-chief of the British Army, the Duke of York reformed and transformed the military service into a modern fighting force.

Inside the hollow column, designed by Benjamin Dean Wyatt, a spiral staircase leads up to a viewing platform at the base of the duke's bronze statue, sculptured by Sir Richard Westmacott. After several people died by suicide after throwing themselves from the top during the mid-1800s the monument was closed to the public. Measuring 124 feet in height, with the duke at the top, when he died in debt it was suggested at the time he was now out of reach of his creditors.

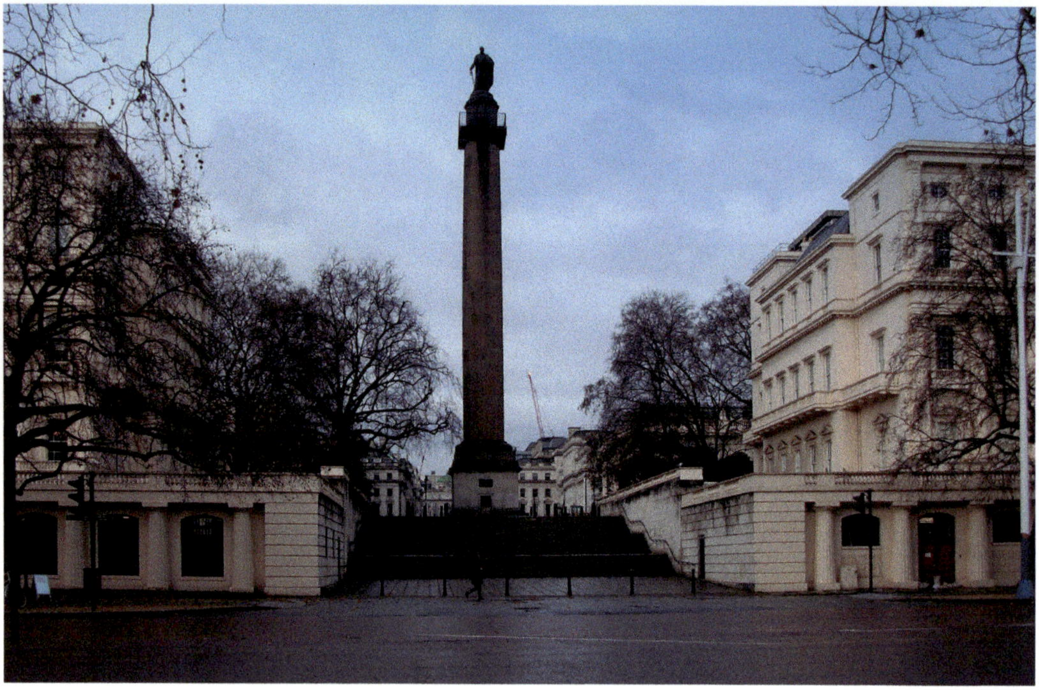

Waterloo Place, SW1.

The duke's debt, however, was nothing compared to government spending supporting the economy during the pandemic: an estimated debt of £62.1 billion in April 2020, £51.1 billion more than the previous year.[1] Covid-19 fundamentally changed people's lives financially and socially, London's population is predicted to fall for the first time this century, the pandemic prompting people to re-evaluate living and working in cities.[2]

With the vaccination rollout underway by February 2021, the government outlined the roadmap towards exiting lockdown. A year on, despite 130 million administered vaccinations in the United Kingdom, many restrictions remained as new virus variants emerged. In January 2022, Transport for London figures showed Tube numbers dropped to 39 per cent of normal,[3] and UKHospitality reported a £115 billion loss to the hospitality industry since the start of the pandemic.[4] Going forward into 2022, the vaccination remains the first line of defence against the virus, and lockdown restrictions were gradually phased out.

London and its people have survived previous catastrophes, plagues, fires, and wars, all of which shaped London as we know it today.

In February 2021, the government outlined the roadmap towards exiting lockdown; however, it remains to be seen what long-term effects lockdown will have had on the city and its people.

1. Public sector finances, UK, Office for National Statistics, January 2021 (ons.gov.uk).
2. PWC, UK Economic Outlook, p. 16, January 2021.
3. *Evening Standard*, p. 1, 7 January 2022.
4. UKHospitality.org.uk, News and Press General, February 2022.

Bibliography

Cook, Mrs E. T., *Highways and Byways in London* (Macmillan, 1902)

Dickens, Charles and Rosalind Vallance, *Dickens' London* (The Folio Society, 1966)

Herber, Mark, *Criminal London* (Phillimore & Co. Ltd, 2002)

Hinnert, Christopher and Ben Weinreb (eds), *The London Encyclopaedia* (Book Club Associates, 1983)

Wheeler, Harold F. B. (ed.), *The Book of Knowledge* (The Waverley Book Company, Ltd)

Websites

Britannica
Gov.uk
Historic UK
Museum of London
National Archives
Old Maps Online
Price Waterhouse Cooper
Victorian Web
Vision of Britain

Acknowledgements

The author would like to thank the Wellcome Collection, London, for use of archive images on pages 8, 11, 12 and 15. If for any reason I have not credited people or organisations as necessary I apologise for any oversight and will make the necessary correction at the first opportunity.

About the Author

Born in Greenwich, London, David Ramzan has always had a keen interest in the history of his home town and studied local history as an undergraduate at the University of Oxford. A self-employed graphic designer, illustrator and artist, he also worked in the special educational needs sector and has written several historical publications and articles for magazines and periodicals, subjects that include local, maritime and football history, piracy, smuggling, and Victorian crime.